EXTREME EARTH

E EARTH

TED SMART

This edition produced for The Book People Ltd, Hall Wood Avenue, Haydock, St Helen's WA11 9UL

First published in 2003 by
Collins, an imprint of
HarperCollinsPublishers
77-85 Fulham Palace Road
Hammersmith
London W6 8JB

The Collins website address is www.collins.co.uk

09	08	07	06	05	04	03
7	6	5	4	3	2	1

This book was conceived, designed and produced by Here+There
Design: Caz Hildebrand
Editorial Director: Joe Dolce
Written by George W. Stone; captions by Hugo Davenport
Picture Editor: Lily Richards
Research Editor: Nathaniel Harris
Copy Editor: Margaret Yamashita
Proofreader: Catharine Browne

Thanks to Denise Bates, Claire Conville, Jonathan Burnham, Lisa John, Mark Lewis, Kate Marlow, Julie Martin, Mary Parvin, Mark Paton, Gerald Sealy, Patrick Walsh

A catalogue record for this book is available from the British Library

ISBN 0-00-769005-3
Colour separations by Saxon Photolitho, Norwich
Printed and bound in Singapore

'Civilization exists by geological consent, subject to change without notice'

Will Durant, 1885–1981

CONTENTS

Simon Winchester

INTROD

We have a plan, my son and I. One day we will meet at the lake that lies at the base of the southern slopes of what is unarguably the most important mountain in the world.

We will travel there from the two ends of the pilgrims' routes. He will head west from Peking, and will battle his way through the mountains of western Szechuan and Xinjiang, across the gorges of the Yangtze, the Mekong and the Salween, up onto the plains of Tibet. Eventually he will find his way to the deep-blue and ice-cold waters of what millions know as Lake Mansarovar.

I will come north to meet him from India. I will cross the Himalaya by way of the six-kilometre-high pass via which all bare-footed mendicants are supposed to travel, and I will find myself high in the windy Tibetan plateau too, heading north. In due course – we have agreed that we shall go on foot, not on the hands and knees that the most dedicated of acolytes are known to employ – I will get to Mansarovar too.

And there will be my son, I have no doubt. We shall shake hands and gaze around us, and then look up to our north to feast our eyes and souls on the sight of the snowbound slopes of the holiest of all the world's peaks, which the Buddhists and Sikhs and Hindus and not a few Christians know also as Meru, but which geographers and the outside world know as Mount Kailash. It is a peak of extraordinary, breathtakingly unusual shape. It rises, majestic in its solitude, like an immense snow-covered fist rising clear up to the stars. The Tibetan plain is the closest of all the earth to heaven, they say. And Mount Kailash is the ladder by which one reaches God.

In our family we have always liked the world's extremes, of one kind or another. When I was young I had a fixation with finding the source of all rivers, and my now-Kailash-directed son recalls with distaste how one foggy and sleeting New Year's Day 30 years ago I dragged him and his grumbling brothers across miles of muddy fields to the gravel depression deep in a Cotswold wood where the River Thames is said to have its true beginning. And during their teenage years I dragged all three of the boys to the highest peaks in the Kingdom – to Snowdon in Wales (via the dreaded knife-edged ridge of slate known as Crib Goch, the teetering, heart-racing passage that later became a family test of bravery or foolhardiness, or both), to the top of Ben Nevis in Scotland (via the similarly awful granite blade called the Carn mor Dearg arête), and to the summit of Scafell Pike in the Lake District, the relatively modest mountain that is the best that England can offer.

But there have been more ambitious expeditions, too. Maybe I was predestined to have a fondness for the lonely and the far away, but it was my years at Oxford that finally infected me properly. My professor there was a mountaineer named Lawrence Wager, who had climbed the then still unconquered Everest to 8,235 metres, and had a love for the world's wilder places. He urged me to go to East Greenland, and with five friends I spent a long, cold summer high on the ice cap south of a settlement called Scoresbysund. We had all manner of adventures there – we were socked in by bad weather, had to hunt for food (including, heaven forbid, having to shoot a polar bear) and were forced to walk for days across a mile-deep sea on a maze of thin and ever-shifting ice floes.

I've been in love with Greenland from that summer on, and have been back a score of times. To me it represents some kind of frontier that separates the soft comfort of the world that I know from the harder and less yielding realities of another that I yearn to understand. Once I had a West Greenland Inuit take me on his dogsled, miles from any settlement or hunters' route, and leave me, quite alone, for a couple of weeks. There was nothing but the immense quiet of the high Arctic: not a bird, not a creature, not a sound – not even the wind, since whatever blew had nothing to blow against, except for me and my little tent. I prayed so hard for the man to reappear to take me home; and yet once I was

For me the joy of extremes is the joy of silent awe.

swishing back through the snow with him, I found myself wishing that he hadn't come at all.

For me the joy of extremes is the joy of silent awe. I am not infused by the kind of death wish that makes others pit themselves against the world's extremes, to tempt them to do their worst and be bold or brave or cunning enough to meet their challenges and come up winning. I am instead a soft-handed and uncourageous man, eager only to gaze, and to gasp in amazement at the wonder of it all. And there is wonder aplenty – in my life, and in the pages that follow, for a whole generation of astonishment.

I like the lonely places, for example. I love Turfan in China, Tannu-Tuva near Mongolia, Weihaiwei in Manchuria – places that are forgotten, passed by, overlooked, rarely seen today. I love islands that are similarly overlooked: I am drawn to Pitcairn in the Pacific Ocean and Tristan da Cunha in the Atlantic; and barren rocks like Kerguelen and Amsterdam and Jan Mayen, less frequently visited still, foggy holdouts in the cold and stormy waters of even higher latitudes. In all of these places there are men (and a small number of women) whose qualities of endurance and stoicism, of boatmanship and storytelling, of independence and initiative and resourcefulness, are unlike anything that we know in the cosy worlds that most of us inhabit today. The people of these extremely sited islands are examples of mankind *as I like to think we used to be*: visiting them today is a powerful reminder – a sobering reminder, too – of the once-vital sense of human nobility, and of how it has evaporated, slowly but steadily, under the beguiling influence of regular food and central heat.

The most beautiful places, too, can be sobering to see. The loveliest of all the world's volcanoes, for instance – and by *lovely* one means I suppose, *the most perfectly*

symmetrical – is Mayon, in the Philippines. It is not especially big, nor has it killed as many as Krakatoa, for example, which is high on any list of the world's extremes: but it is a mountain so splendid and majestic as to inspire, even from many miles' distance, an unmatchable awe.

A friend and I climbed it once: we started long before dawn, hacking through the thick pandanus groves at its base; we reached the smooth and slippery andesite cliffs, running with small snakes, by breakfast; we were on the treacherous ash-slopes of the summit cone by 11; and then a furious storm broke on us, and our guides scattered like frightened children, and took to whimpering in a cave. We crawled on through a hailstorm that was blown horizontal by the ferocious winds, and we reached the sulphur-crusted edge of the cauldron by noon. And just then the wind dropped, the cloud blew raggedly away – and all the Philippines stretched a hundred miles away into a bluest of blue distances. It was silent; we were alone; we were at the edge of the world, at the intersection of the unknown elemental earth and the unreal pleasures to which, in a few minutes, we would be returning. But for that one second, all was sublime.

And then there are those places that combine the dangerously beautiful with the splendours of isolation, the places that manage to conjoin solitude with magic. Close to where I have a cottage, in the western isles of Scotland, is one of the world's greatest whirlpools. In the planet's seas there are five giant tidal dislocations which each cause the local waters to swirl in an immense and terribly dangerous vortex: two are in Norway (the infamous *Maelstrom* being one of them), one is in Japan, one rather smaller version is on a water boundary between Maine and New Brunswick on North America's eastern shores – and one is mine, five sea miles from where I live, in the strait of water between the little-

> We were at the edge of the world, at the intersection of the unknown elemental earth and the unreal pleasures to which, in a few minutes, we would be returning.

known island of Scarba and its better-known neighbour of Jura (which is where George Orwell wrote *1984*).

The strait, and thus the whirlpool, is called Corryvreckan; and when the tides are running and vast overfalls hit a submerged pinnacle of rock that rises to within 60 feet of an otherwise deep black channel, a watery hell breaks loose. The water swirls and roars and sends pillars of spray high into the air, and it makes a growling sound that can be heard on Colonsay, 20 miles away. Even well-found boats are advised not to attempt passage through the Strait of Corryvreckan when a spring tide is running: once in a while a passing ship may toss trees into the vortex, to see what happens – they vanish forever, dragged down hundreds of feet and smashed into pulp by the relentless force of the sea.

Corryvreckan instills a profound sense of awe – though not, it must be admitted, in the silent environment in which awe is best experienced. I first saw the whirlpool from one of the cliffs of southern Scarba: at first the sea was still, since the tide was slack. Then the race began, and soon the waters began to roil and rage, and within half an hour the spume was rising like smoke and the cannonading roar had started, and the waters below looked like the base of Niagara, white with foam and huge with sound. Then, out of the side of my eye, I saw something: it was a roe deer, young and frightened, but standing beside me transfixed as I was. He saw me look at him, gazed back at me for one terrified instant – then took a further look at the raging sea below the pair of us, and dashed off into the heather, back to the safety of the world he knew.

For this is what these extreme places mean – at least to me. They are a vision of the world I want to know, glimpsed from the safety of the world of which I am at least reasonably aware. From time to time, if the journey is not too difficult and doesn't require too much by way of heroics, I sample these places: I sail to Tristan and clamber onshore, I climb Mayon and peer into the crater's heart, I take a well-found boat (as I now have on three occasions) through the whirlpool of Corryvreckan when the tide is in full spate. But usually I gaze from afar, and allow the full essential majesty of their existence to wash over me. I let each of them serve as a reminder of the infinitesimal scale of all that is human, and the indescribable and utterly impressive wonderment of the world and the universe beyond.

Nowhere, I believe, is that wonderment likely to be more dramatically on offer than at Mount Kailash. I have not been there, not yet. I only know what I have read, and heard from some of the few who have visited, and who have accomplished their visitation as pilgrims should, on foot. (It is possible to get to Kailash by motor car– a journey I think of as no better than spiritual vandalism.) In a few years' time my son and I will meet there, and we will gaze up and try to see if we can spy what many a pilgrim has said is visible in the glacial cracks of the upper slopes – a giant *swastik*, a holy mark, something that suggests, if only symbolically, that this is indeed a sacred place, worthy of all the importance and the status that it commands.

I daresay that we shall stay beside the shore of Lake Mansarovar until we see this sign; and then my son and I will leave this most spiritually extreme of all the world's wild places, and we will travel back home, together, entirely fulfilled. And after Kailash, I begin to wonder, will there truly be anywhere else to go. *Oh yes*, my son will say: we have only just begun to explore the rest of the world, and all of its vast empires of wonder that remain.

.EAI

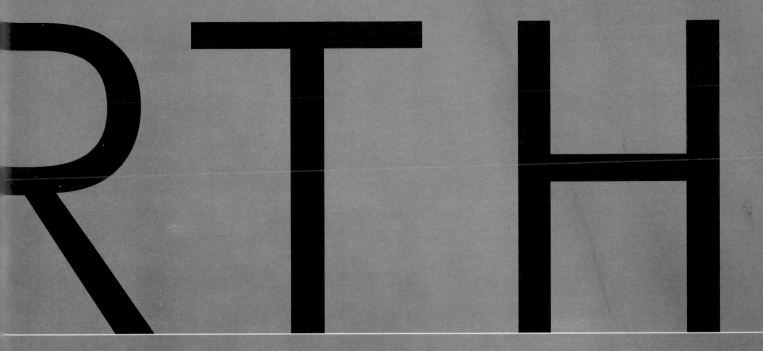

'As we drove past the cemetery in Yungay the car began to shake. We immediately got out and I saw several homes as well as a small bridge crossing a creek near Cemetery Hill collapse. After a half minute the shaking began to subside ... and I heard a great roar coming from Huascarán. Looking up, I saw what appeared to be a wave, a cloud of dust, and it looked as though a large mass of rock and ice was breaking loose from the north peak. My immediate reaction was to run for the high ground of Cemetery Hill 200 metres away.

'The crest of the wave had a curl, like a huge breaker coming in from the ocean, at least 80 metres high. I reached the upper level of the cemetery just as the debris flow struck the base of the hill. I was probably only 10 seconds ahead of it.'

— Mateo Casaverde, a Peruvian geophysicist, eyewitness to the Huascarán
earthquake and avalanche

EARTH'S HIGHEST POINT

Mount Everest
Location: Central Himalaya, on the border of Tibet and Nepal
Total Height: 8,850 m
Coordinates: 27° 59′ 00″ N | 86° 56′ 00″ E

"Because it is there." This was the explanation of legendary climber George Leigh Mallory for his attempts to climb to the top of Mount Everest, Earth's "third pole" and the only one left unconquered at the time of his expeditions. At that time, it was thought that no man could endure the thin air, frigid temperatures, and billowy wind gusts long enough to reach the world's highest peak. But Mallory was stubborn, and when he perished in 1924 on his third attempt to climb to the top of Chomolangma (what Tibetan Sherpas call their "goddess mother of the snows"), his fate confirmed that the rooftop of the world was no place for humans.

Not until May 28, 1953, did a New Zealand beekeeper, Edmund Hillary, and his Sherpa guide, Tenzing Norgay, finally conquer Sagarmatha, the Nepalese "sky head", and enter the history books. Theirs was the ninth attempt to reach the top of Mount Everest. Since then, roughly 1,100 climbers have equalled their feat, and at least 170 others have died trying.

The official height of Everest, 8,850 metres, was announced on November 11, 1999. This figure, 2.1 metres higher than the previously accepted measurement, was determined by using satellite-based Global Positioning System technology. A team of seven climbers measured the mountain from the summit, collecting data from various GPS satellite receivers at the very top. It is believed that the actual peak of Everest is buried under as many as 6 metres of permanent ice; future tests will confirm this.

Mount Everest crowns the young and still-growing Himalaya, the mountain range atop the Indian plate that began its upward thrust some 25 million years ago. The Himalaya still is rising about 5 ceentimetres a year. Although Everest has been Earth's highest peak for only about half a million years, its appeal to some – and its cold indifference to most others – has never been equalled.

Known in Tibet as Chomolangma, or goddess mother of the snows, and in Nepal as Sagarmatha, mother of the universe, Mount Everest has seen more than 150 climbers die on her icy slopes. Yet still they come, alone or without oxygen, like Austria's Reinhold Meissner; others ski down, as Yuicho Miura of Japan did in 1970.

EARTH'S HIGHEST LANDMASS

Plateau of Tibet
Location: South-west China
Height above sea level: 4,000 to 5,500 m
Coordinates: 33° 00′ 00″ N | 92° 00′ 00″ E

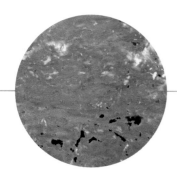

The Plateau of Tibet stretches across south-west China, covering an area about half that of the lower 48 United States and bounded by the deserts of the Tarim and Qaidam to the north and the Himalayan, Karakoram, and Pamir mountain chains to the south and west.

With an elevation of nearly 5 kilometres above sea level, this desolate, dry, windswept landscape is the world's highest plateau. Although its highest mountain elevations don't surpass 7,010 metres, the plateau does contain other earth extremes in the folds of its coarse and varied terrain, widespread permafrost, and numerous salt lakes. Nepal's Tilicho, for example, is one of the highest lakes in the world, with a surface elevation of 4,920 metres.

Plateaus are one of four major landforms, along with mountains, hills, and plains. Upward movement of the earth's crust, caused by the crashing of tectonic plates, forms flat, tabletop-like plateaus. Over time, weathering and erosion sculpt these landforms, while rivers carve out valleys from the caprock, etching steep sides or cliffs around what is now a plateau.

The Plateau of Tibet began to be formed in the early Miocene epoch and most likely reached its present elevation about 8 million years ago. Regions within and around it encompass sweeping steppes, turquoise lakes, dense forests, and deserts, and support such endangered animals as wild yaks, Saiga and Tibetan antelopes, Himalayan black bears, sheep, and rhinoceroses.

Roughly 50 million years ago the Eurasian plate crashed into the Indian plate, creating the spectacular terrain of the Himalaya and the Plateau of Tibet. The region around the "rooftop of the world" is constantly changing under earth forces strong enough to force the Himalayan range skyward by a few centimetres each year. Around these peaks are some of the world's most remarkable geological features, from snowy mountains and glaciers to canyon ranges and tropical rain forests.

In his classic *Seven Years in Tibet,* Heinrich Harrer wrote: 'It took all our energy to collect yak dung and find water, and even talking was a waste of strength. Once a day we cooked meat and ladled the gravy straight out of the simmering saucepan. One could do that here without fear of scalding one's tongue as the boiling point was so low.'

George C. Band

ASCENT

I was perched delicately on a 45-degree ice slope at close to 8,235 metres, trying to hack out a ledge for our tiny two-man tent with my ice axe. I hit rock at the back — the ledge was far too narrow — so when we rigged the tent it sagged alarmingly over the edge. Our support team descended, and Joe Brown and I were left on our own. We drew lots to see who would sleep along the outside edge. I lost.

It was May 24, 1955. Joe and I had been chosen by Charles Evans to have the first crack at the summit of Kangchenjunga. At 10,000 metres, it was then the world's highest unclimbed peak, only about 250 metres lower than Everest but considered more difficult. Over the years, it had defeated very strong expeditions on both the north-east spur and the north-west face, and frequent avalanches raked the south-west face. John Hunt, fresh from leading the first ascent of Everest in 1953, when Hillary and Tenzing reached the summit shortly before the Queen's coronation, said that "Kangch", as we called it, "would be the greatest feat in mountaineering". He also said the climb would involve technical problems and dangers even greater than those we had encountered on Everest.

On Everest I was the youngest member of our team, and played a relatively modest role, so this climb was my chance to shine. Joe was on his first visit to the Himalayas, but his reputation as Britain's finest rock climber preceded him. Everest had been climbed several times within 300 metres of its summit before ultimate success. But we were trying the largely virgin south-west face of Kangch, where no one had ever surpassed 6,000 metres. Our objective was to reach the Great Shelf — a prominent ice terrace at 7,300 metres. Just in case things proved easier than expected we took oxygen and sufficient equipment to attack on the summit.

This climb had one unusual feature: the eastern half of the mountain lies in the Indian state of Sikkim, where the people regard Kangchenjunga as a god. It was sacrilege to desecrate its summit, so we promised not to pass the point from which we could see an easy route to the top. We would not tread on the summit itself.

Over four weeks we devised a route that bypassed a treacherous lower ice fall and kept to the central cliffs of a steep upper ice fall where we were relatively safe from avalanches. After setting up camps and escorting Sherpa teams carrying supplies, we were ready to launch the assault in pairs on successive days: first Joe and me, then Norman Hardie and Tony Streather.

That night Joe and I made a lemon drink from crystals and tea with lots of sugar to prevent dehydration. Supper was asparagus soup from a packet, a small tin of lambs' tongues with dehydrated mashed potatoes, and a nightcap of drinking chocolate. Then we crawled into our sleeping bags wearing every scrap of clothing we had, even our boots. We didn't want them getting frozen stiff like Hillary's on Everest. We kept on our climbing rope and anchored it to a nearby rock spike in case the tent slid off the ledge. We shared a cylinder of sleeping oxygen at 1 litre per minute each, but I didn't sleep well – I was too excited. The others had done their utmost to get us so high and we didn't want to let them down. I prayed for good weather.

By 8.15am we were climbing the icy Gangway leading to the West Ridge. There were tricky pinnacles on the ridge, so we planned to turn off the Gangway and tackle the face directly. Because the ground was a mixture of ice, snow, and rock, we took off our crampons and treated it more like a rock climb. We aimed for a little subsidiary snow ridge that led back up to the West Ridge, then climbed to a sensational rocky eyrie on which we were poised mid-air, thousands of feet above the shelf and glacier below.

We reached the ridge at 2pm with only a couple of hours of oxygen left.
"We should turn back by 3pm, Joe," I said, "or we may have to spend the night out."
"We've got to reach the top before then," he yelled back.

Keeping just below the ridge to avoid the wind, we came up beneath a nose of rock that reared up, sheer and smooth. The wall was broken by several vertical cracks about 6-metres tall, with a slight overhang at the top. Joe was keen to try one. With his oxygen turned to the

There was a sea of cloud at 6,000 metres, with only the highest peaks standing out like rocky islands in a sea of white waves.

full 6 litres per minute, and safeguarding his lead with a couple of running belays, he forced his way up and I followed.

Before us, some 6 metres away and 1.5 metres above the ground on which we stood, was the very top, formed by a gently sloping cone of snow. We had come as far as we were allowed.

Many people have asked whether I was tempted to tread those last few feet. The answer is no: I was very tired and glad for any excuse to stop. But what a view! There was a sea of cloud at 6,000 metres, with only the highest peaks standing out like rocky islands in a sea of white waves. To the west, 130 kilometres away, the giants Makalu, Lhotse and Everest were silhouetted deep blue against the faint horizon.

We turned to descend. After an hour the oxygen was finished, so we discarded the sets and climbed down wearily. Guided by shouts from Hardie and Streather, we reached our tent as darkness fell. We should have continued down, but the dark made the journey too dangerous. So the four of us squeezed into the tiny tent and again I found myself on the outside edge.

Hardie and Streather successfully repeated our climb the next day. Being more practised at climbing ice than rock, they kept their crampons on. They didn't like the look of Joe's vertical crack near the top and instead carried on around the corner, where they found an easy snow ridge running up to the summit. But they also stopped short, out of respect for the god of Kangchenjunga. No one climbed the mountain again for 22 years.

EARTH'S HIGHEST MOUNTAIN RANGE

The Himalaya
Location: Northern border of the Indian subcontinent
Coordinates: 28° 00′ 00″ N | 84° 00′ 00″ E

Roughly 55 million years ago, when the Indian tectonic plate began to collide with the Eurasian tectonic plate – advancing more than 2,012 kilometres into Asia and still moving today, though more slowly – it began squeezing upward the light sedimentary rock of the ancient Tethys Sea. About 25 million years ago, these crumpled rocks gave rise to the Himalaya, a Sanskrit term (meaning "abode of snow") that encompasses three distinct mountain ranges spanning some 2,500 kilometres on the southern fringe of the Plateau of Tibet.

The Himalaya contain more than 30 peaks higher than 7,620 metres and all 14 of the world's peaks over 8,000 metres, including the world's highest, Mount Everest (8,850 metres), and third-highest, Kanchenjunga (8,586 metres). This relatively young and still-growing mountain system is subject to severe earthquakes and extreme influxes of mountaineers who dream of conquering at least one of its summits. More spiritual visitors are drawn here to make pilgrimages to Hindu shrines or to connect with Tibetan Buddhist belief systems at monasteries. Trekkers take on the foothills of the Himalaya, the extensively glaciated southern slopes feeding the Indian subcontinent's major rivers, including the Indus, Sutlej, Ganges, and Zangbo-Brahmaputra.

The Himalaya are the source of many myths, from Tibetan folk tales to Buddhist legends to simple village superstitions. Paradise is a prevalent theme, and one appropriate at such high altitudes. Shambhala, one place of universal wisdom and peace, is said to be located somewhere beyond Tibet. Some people refer to this mythical kingdom of jewel-like lakes, wish-fulfilling trees, and speaking stones as Shangri-La. While many visitors scoff at the notion that heaven is somewhere in Tibet – the Chinese government especially would be quick to deny such a possibility – to believers, Shambhala is, if not just around the bend, very close.

Hindu sages say the Himalaya are made of solid granite. Every 1,000 years a bird flies over them with a scarf in its beak, brushing the peaks as it passes. When they have thus been worn away, one day of a cosmic cycle will have elapsed.

EARTH'S LONGEST LAND MOUNTAIN RANGE

Andes
Location: South America
Total Length: 8,900 km
Coordinates: 20° 00′ 00″ S | 67° 00′ 00″ W

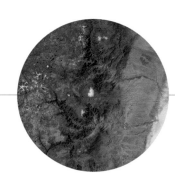

The sharp features, high icy peaks, and deep-green folds of the Andes reveal this mountain chain's youth, but no single picture could ever do justice to the length and variety of the world's longest mountain chain above sea level. Paralleling the Pacific Ocean from the southernmost Tierra del Fuego archipelago, north through seven South American countries, the 8,900-kilometre-long Andes mountain chain forms the backbone of this continent.

The Andes are rising quickly, accompanied by volcanoes and earthquakes. About 25 million years ago, the eastward-moving Nazca plate squeezed beneath the South American continent, pushing up the land above it while smashing and shifting layers of solid rock. The Andes are moving upward at a rate of about 30.5 centimetres every 300 years and constitute the second-tallest mountain range after the Himalaya. The highest peak in the Andes (and in the Western Hemisphere) is Aconcagua, which rises 6,960 metres on the Argentine-Chilean border. Runoff from the Cordillera Real range feeds Lake Titicaca, the world's highest navigable body of water, with 8,290 square kilometres of surface. Andean waters are the source of great rivers like the Amazon, the Orinoco, and the Río de la Plata.

Beyond peaks, lakes, and rivers, the Andes contain other extremes, including the high, cold Atacama Desert in north-central Chile, the driest place in the world, and plateaus and valleys that sustained some of the hemisphere's earliest native civilizations. The Inca, who left behind the remarkable city of Machu Picchu in the Peruvian Andes, nurtured their culture in this range. Other residents include the Pukara, who lived in the Andean highlands more than 2,500 years before the Inca, the Tiwanaku, and the Chavin of the first millennium B.C.E. in Peru, and in many ways paved the way for the Incas.

Note that although the Andes comprise the earth's longest *land* mountain range, the Mid-Atlantic Ridge, which crosses the globe underwater from the Arctic to the Atlantic, passing through the Indian Ocean to the Pacific, is actually the world's longest mountain range, four times longer than the Andes, Rockies, and Himalaya combined.

EARTH'S TALLEST AND BIGGEST MOUNTAINS

Mauna Kea: 9,754 m high from the ocean floor
Coordinates: Mauna Kea: 19° 49′ 25″ N | 155° 28′ 15″ W
Mauna Loa: 9,661 m high | 80,000 km^3 in volume | 5,271 km^2 in area
Coordinates: Mauna Loa: 19° 28′ 56″ N | 155° 36′ 18″ W
Location: Hawaii, island of Hawaii (Big Island)

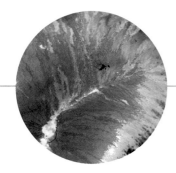

Trick question: What's the tallest mountain on earth? Most people answer Mount Everest. At 8,850 metres, Everest is, in fact, earth's highest peak and highest land elevation. But it is not the tallest or even the biggest mountain. These distinctions go to two neighbouring seamounts on Hawaii's Big Island, which is made up of five volcanoes that have run together to form a single island. Measured from its base at the bottom of the Pacific Ocean, the dormant volcano Mauna Kea (opposite page, foreground), rises an astonishing 9,754 metres, of which 4,205 metres are above sea level. If Mauna Kea were on, literally, an equal footing with Everest, its peak would be nearly a mile higher – and far beyond the reach of any climber. Where mass is concerned, Everest again comes up short: Mauna Loa

(opposite page, background), is 93 metres shorter than Mauna Kea (still a tall 9,661 metres), but its 80,000 cubic kilometres of mass makes it, far and away, earth's most massive mountain.

On top of this – literally – Mauna Loa is one of the world's most active volcanoes. It has erupted four times (in 1942, 1949, 1975, and 1984) since its period of greatest activity in 1881, and its expanse could grow with future eruptions and lava flows.

Hawaii Volcanoes National Park houses Mauna Loa and the Kilauea Crater, and Mauna Kea is about 48 kilometres north, but the two behemoths are not connected by a direct route. To get around the Big Island, you have to cross terrain that ranges from desert to rain forest to erupting volcano.

'Mountains are earth's undecaying monuments.'

Nathaniel Hawthorne

EARTH'S HIGHEST FREESTANDING MOUNTAIN

Mount Kilimanjaro
Location: Tanzania
Height: 5,895 m
Coordinates: 03° 05' S | 37° 21' E

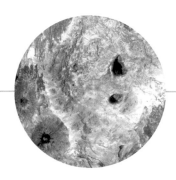

In the foreground of a classic photograph of Mount Kilimanjaro, Masai herdsmen stand in the savannah near Amboseli National Park in Tanzania. Rising behind them from the flat plains is a snowcapped massif of unquestionable beauty. Kilimanjaro is the tallest mountain in Africa and the highest freestanding mountain in the world. Located 3° south of the equator in north-eastern Tanzania, it is the largest in a belt of about 20 volcanoes near the southern end of the East African Rift Valley. This immense mountain – actually a recently extinct volcano (although steam and sulphur are still streaming out) – is made up of three volcanic masses. It's called Oldoinyo Oibor ("white mountain" in Masai) and Kilima Njaro ("shining mountain" in Swahili), but if you intend to climb to the top, to Uhuru peak (5,895 metres),

the word you should keep in mind is *polepole*, which is Swahili for "slowly".

Kilimanjaro may be the easiest of the world's seven summits to climb, but the experience is still a gruelling one that delivers you to the top of the African continent, above a layer of clouds and alongside ancient bluish glaciers. The mountain's slopes are gentle and forgiving up to a point. The final third of the hike is up a steep grade, with the howling wind and hot sun always in force. It can take six days to reach Kilimanjaro's summit and another two to descend. The view from the top, however, is worth every hardship. Craters large and small abound – cold, rocky, and brown – and the terrain looks simultaneously ancient and raw.

EARTH'S LARGEST TABLE MOUNTAINS

Guyana Highlands, Cerro (Pico) de la Neblina
Location: Border between Venezuela and Brazil
Total Size: 446 km long | average width 16 km | 1.6 km deep
Coordinates: 23° 15' 00" S | 49° 30' 00" W

Tepuis are flat-topped, sheer-walled table mountains that tower over the rugged savannahs and forests of Venezuela. To explorers and botanists, tepuis are fragile ecosystems that support orchids, lichens, ferns, succulents, and millions of other rain-forest plants, scores of them never seen before.

More than 100 tepuis sprawl across the Guyana Highlands at the border between Brazil and Venezuela. The summits of the tepuis are nutrient-poor, cool, and soggy, an environment that would seem to promise little in the way of biodiversity. But surprisingly, tepuis hosts four distinct vegetation zones, starting at the base and proceeding to the talus slope, the base of the cliff, and finally the summit. Along the way to the top, monkeys, sloths, weasels, jaguars, pumas, bats, snakes, iguanas, and a huge number of birds remind hikers that this is indeed a very wild zone.

Tepuis rest on the Guyana Shield, a rock basement that was formed over a billion years ago. Over time, this granitic basement was overlaid with sand that was compressed and cemented until it was several thousand metres thick. About 180 million years ago, uplifting and erosion separated and isolated the tepuis, remnants of highly weathered parent rock that are among the oldest geological formations in South America.

'How shall I ever forget the solemn mystery of it? The height of the trees and the thickness of the boles ... vivid orchids and wonderful coloured lichens ... the effect was as a dream of fairyland.'

A tepui as described in *The Lost World* by Sir Arthur Conan Doyle

EARTH'S MOST SPECTACULAR VERTICAL ROCK FACES

El Capitan, Yosemite National Park, California, U.S.A.
Coordinates: 37° 52' 00" N | 119° 24' 00" W

Devil's Tower National Monument, Wyoming, U.S.A.
Coordinates: 44° 35' 21" N | 104° 41' 46" W

Trollrygen, Romsdal region, Norway
Coordinates: 62° 40' 00" N | 07° 50' 00" E

The Thumbnail, Torssukatak Fjord, Greenland
Coordinates: 69° 58' 00" N | 51° 05' 00" W

The vertical monolith known as Devil's Tower, in Wyoming, rises 264 metres above the meandering Belle Fourche River to create a stunning, square-walled, flat-topped terrace resembling a massive stone tree trunk. Scientists believe that Devil's Tower formed when magma filled the core of a volcano, forging a dense column of basalt that hardened into a plug of rock. After millions of years of erosion by wind and rain, the volcano weathered away, sculpting the cliffs into this solid rock core. This monolith is a sacred site for many Northern Plains Indians, who have many names for this rock uprising, including Mateo Tepee ("Bear Lodge"). The legend about the creation of Devil's Tower is that a fearsome bear chased people onto this rock, which miraculously rose, lifting them to safety and leaving the bear in the dust.

In California's Yosemite National Park, El Capitan, the world's largest granite monolith, (right) rises almost 1000 metres above the valley floor and attracts expert climbers by the hundreds. A far more remote and tantalizing challenge is the Thumbnail, the world's highest sea cliff and one of the highest vertical rock faces, extending 1,500 metres straight up from the Torssukatak Fjord in southernmost Greenland. The highest sea cliff of all is a flat wall that peaks well above the clouds. Another monstrous vertical rock wall is located near the small fjord town of Andelsnes, on Norway's west coast. This huge gneiss cliff rises vertically more than 1,100 metres and is named Trollrygen ("Troll Wall") in honor of the spires and pinnacles decorating the rim of its summit. Legend has it that the trolls who once inhabited this coastal mountain region (some say they still do) were petrified forever for their sins.

EARTH'S HIGHEST MOUNTAINS

1 EVEREST | HIMALAYAS,NEPAL/TIBET | 8,850 m
2 K2 (GODWIN AUSTEN) | KARAKORAM, PAKISTAN/CHINA | 8,611 m
3 KANCHENJUNGA | HIMALAYAS, INDIA/NEPAL | 8,586 m
4 LHOTSE I | HIMALAYAS, NEPAL/TIBET | 8,516 m
5 MAKALU I | HIMALAYAS, NEPAL/TIBET | 8,463 m
6 CHO OYU | HIMALAYAS, NEPAL/TIBET | 8,201 m

All height measurements given in metres, and are correct according to the Columbia Gazetteer of the World and the Merriam Webster Geographical Dictionary. Place names verified through the United States Board on Geographic Names and the National Imagery Mapping Agency's (NIMA) geographic names database.

1   2   3   4   5   6

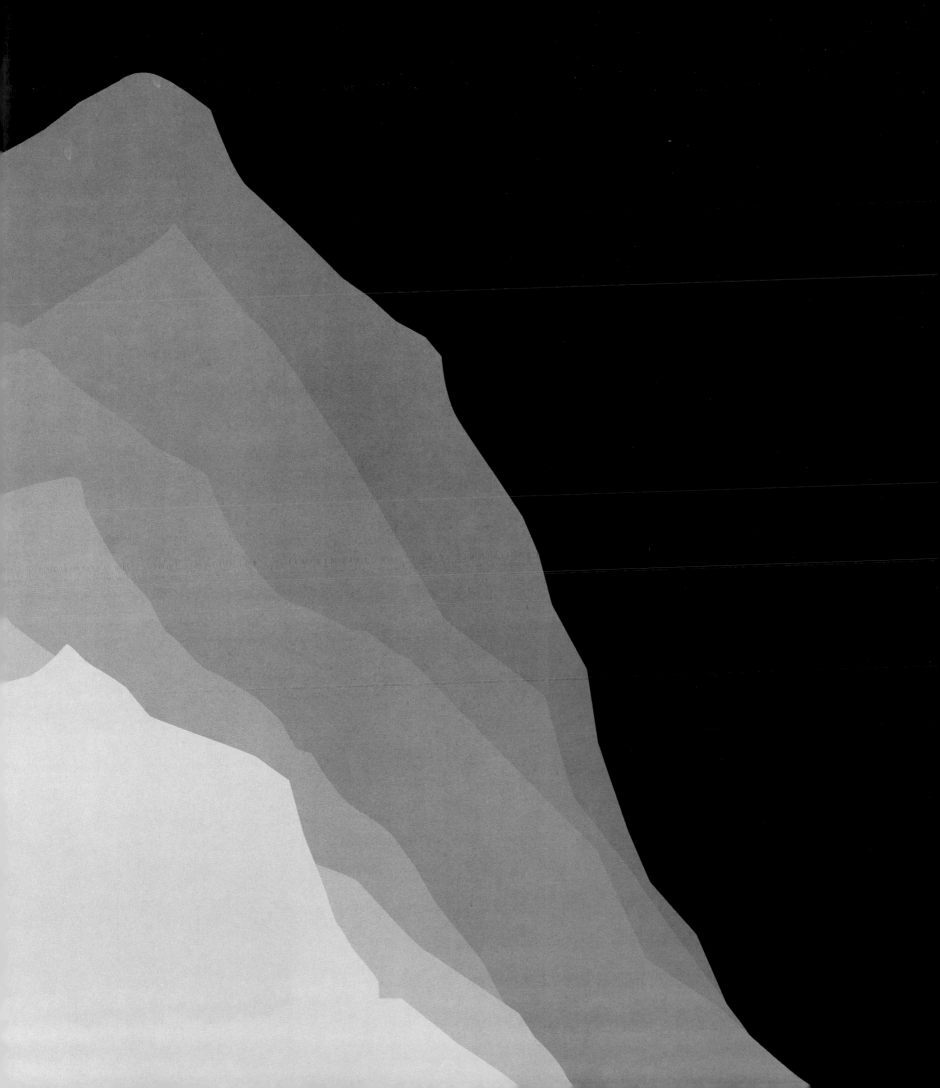

EARTH'S MOST MAGNIFICENT MONOLITH

Uluru
Location: Northern Territory, Australia
Coordinates: 25° 20' 00" S | 131° 00' 00" E

The story that's told to the tourists, and to Australian schoolchildren, is that Uluru is the largest monolith in the world. A "monolith" is a single, massive stone, so Uluru (also known as Ayers Rock) is supposedly a giant pebble either sitting on or partly buried in the desert sand. But geologists say that this is wrong.

The explorer W. C. Gosse sighted Uluru on July 19, 1873. He wrote, "The hill as I approached presented a most peculiar appearance, the upper portion being covered with holes or caves. When I got clear of the sand hills, and was only two miles distant, and glimpsing the hill for the first time, coming fairly into view, what was my astonishment to find it was one immense rock rising abruptly from the plain; the holes I had noticed were caused by the water in some places forming immense caves." Uluru is indeed impressive, rising more than 300 metres above the surrounding desert sands, with a circumference greater than 8 kilometres. Gosse gave Uluru the name of Ayers Rock, after Sir Henry Ayers, the premier of South Australia at that time.

Uluru, whose name is roughly translated as "mother of the earth", is made of sand and gravel laid down about 550 million years ago. Local legend has it that it was created by two boys who carved the mountain out of soil that had softened in the rain. The holes, furrows, and pits in the rock are held to be the scars of battles between animal-like ancestors. Less romantically, it was formed over a period of 100 million years (about 300 million to 400 million years ago), when the landmass containing the future Uluru collided with other continents — leading to folding, faulting, and uplift. This slow-motion collision squeezed the sand and gravel sediments into rock and also tipped them on their side. Then the raised areas mostly eroded away for the next few 100 million years. Around 65 million years ago, everything got wetter. Rivers ran in the area, and sediments filled up the valleys between Uluru, Kata Tjuta, and Mount Connor, smoothing out the landscape. Not much has happened, geologically speaking, over the last 65 million years except more erosion.

Is Uluru the world's biggest monolith? No, Mount Augustus in Western Australia is bigger. Nor is Uluru a giant isolated boulder, half buried in the red desert sand. Rather, it's part of a huge, mostly underground rock formation about 100 kilometres wide and perhaps 5 kilometres thick. The only three parts visible above the ground are Uluru, the magnificent domes of Kata Tjuta (formerly known as the Olgas), and the forgotten mountain, Mount Connor.

Dr Karl S. Kruszelnicki

In one aboriginal legend, Uluru began as a flat sandhill with a waterhole at the centre. A tribe of snake-totem people settled there, finding food and water in abundance. But one day, the sandhill turned to stone, and so did the

snake people. The boulders that once were women can be seen in a gorge, grouped together as if still sitting in their village, while the men, who were sleeping at the time, are strewn amidst the plain beneath

EARTH'S LARGEST MONOLITH

Mount Augustus
Location: Western Australia
Coordinates: 24° 20′ 00″ S | 116° 53′ 00″ E

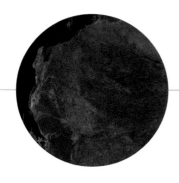

Mount Augustus, which stands 858 metres above the surrounding plain and is 2.5 times the size of Uluru. But unlike its more famous, beautiful cousin, Mount Augustus is covered with vegetation, and so it looks more like a conventional mountain, as opposed to the striking glow of the golden Uluru. Mount Augustus is spectacular in other respects, however. Its central ridge is almost 8 kilometres long, and the monolith's rock is estimated to be 1,000 million years old. Mount Augustus was formed from an uplift that raised and folded an ancient sandstone seabed. As the water receded over hundreds of millions of years, it revealed this sandstone monocline. While Uluru has a hard exterior coating covering its distinctively shaped sandstone body, Mount Augustus slopes gently to its scree foundation. The mountain was named for Sir Augustus Charles Gregory, brother of Francis Gregory, who in 1858 was the first European to climb the monolith.

'Aboriginal creation myths tell of the legendary totemic beings who had wandered over the continent in the Dreamtime, singing out the name of everything that crossed their path – birds, animals, plants, rocks, waterhold – and so singing the world into existence.'

Bruce Chatwin, *The Songlines*

EARTH'S LARGEST NONPOLAR DESERT

Sahara
Location: North Africa
Total Size: 9,065,000 km²
Coordinates: 26° 00′ 00″ N | 13° 00′ 00″ E

The name Sahara comes from the Arabic noun *sahra'*, meaning "desert". But this is one of the few straightforward facts about a desert that is larger than the contiguous United States and covers much of Northern Africa with gravel plains, sand, and dunes.

Although less than a quarter of the desert is covered with sand, the pervasive image of this North African ecosystem is of the wild dunes in its southern area. These dunes, the biggest of which is more than 150 metres high, dominate the terrain. A mysterious phenomenon associated with desert sands is their "singing" or booming, a sound that some dunes emit that is more than a whistle but not quite a song. Some scientists say it has to do with the shape or conductivity of crystalline quartz sand, but the mystery remains unsolved. Contrary to popular imagination, the Sahara also includes shallow, seasonally inundated basins, large oasis depressions, rock-strewn plateaus, and abruptly rising mountains. The highest point is Chad's 3,417-metre Mount Koussi in the Tibesti massif, and its lowest point, 133 metres below sea level, is in Egypt's Qattara Depression.

The desert zones that occupy the northern quarter of Africa span a harsh and unforgiving climate. In most areas, rain can be nearly absent for years and then fall in torrents, which is why you're more likely to drown in the Sahara than in other, wetter places. Vegetation is thin, trade winds are strong and constant, and temperature ranges from freezing to sizzling.

Geologists now think the Sahara actually had a series of wet periods, the most recent occurring 5,000 to 10,000 years ago. But from 3000 B.C.E. onward, Sahara has been arid. Approximately 2 million people inhabit the desert (excluding the Nile Valley); the principal ethnic groups are the Berber-Arab, Tibu, and Tuareg. A romantic quest has always been to travel overland to the fabled city of Timbuktu, in Mali. Synonymous with the ends of the earth, Timbuktu gained its reputation as a city of mystery because until 1828 no European had ever seen it and returned to tell the tale.

'I slept in black tents, blue tents, skin tents, yurts of felt and windbreaks of thorns. One night, caught in a sandstorm in the Western Sahara, I understood Muhammed's dictum, "A journey is a fragment of Hell".' Bruce Chatwin

Sand dunes may evoke the soft curves of the human body, but they can be a harsh, deceptive environment. Found in deserts, on the seabed – even on Mars – they form and reform endlessly, fluid sculptures moulded by the wind. For T.E. Lawrence, in *The Seven Pillars of Wisdom*, the sight of dunes brought relief after a long desert crossing:

'The ground was flat and featureless until five o'clock, when we saw low mounds ahead, and a little later found ourselves in comparative peace, amid sandhills coated slenderly with tamarisk.' In Morocco, meanwhile, the Tuareg tribesmen say that when the wind in the desert stops blowing, it's so quiet that you can hear the earth turn.

EARTH'S LARGEST UNBROKEN EXPANSE OF SAND

The 'Empty Quarter' of the Arabian Desert
Location: Arabian Peninsula
Total Size: 582,750 km²
Coordinates: 25° 00′ 00″ N | 45° 00′ 00″ E

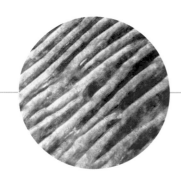

Dry, hot, seemingly endless sand dunes crisscrossed by camels under an unrelenting sun. The popular notion of "desert" is rooted in the south-western Rub' al-Khali ("Empty Quarter"), the massive portion of unbroken sand that makes up a fourth of the nearly 1.6 million-square-kilometre Arabian Desert.

While the gravel plains, rocky highlands, and dunes of the Arabian Desert are fertile ground for the imagination – think of Lawrence of Arabia – the terrain here supports little vegetation. Living conditions are harsh. Constant breezes can quickly become sandstorm gales, and when the sun, which parches the days, retreats into the night sky, freezing temperatures chill the bones.

The Arabian Desert is sparsely populated, but thousands of years ago, the Bedouin and other nomadic peoples learned how to live on the desiccated sands. Archaeologists from the University of Calgary recently have been unearthing a 3,000-year-old temple in Yemen, opening a new door to southern Arabia's ancient civilizations. This find could prove as significant as the ruins of Pompeii, the pyramids of Giza, or the Acropolis of Athens. The Mahram Bilqis (or Temple of the Moon God), buried under the sands of the southern Arabian desert, is believed to have been used throughout the reign of the legendary Queen of Sheba. One archaeologist remarked that "in many respects, the Queen of Sheba's kingdom was the cradle of the Arab civilization and the Mahram Bilqis was at the very heart of this kingdom. Mahram Bilqis may well be considered the eighth wonder of the world."

'A cloud gathers, the rain falls, men live; the cloud disperses without rain, and men and animals die. In the deserts of southern Arabia there is no rhythm of the seasons, no rise and fall of sap, but empty wastes where only the changing temperature marks the passage of the year.'

Wilfred Thesiger, *Arabian Sands*, 1959

EARTH'S OLDEST DESERT

Namib Desert
Location: Namibia, southern Africa
Age: 55 million years old
Coordinates: 23° 00' 00" S | 15° 00' 00" E

In the local Nama language, Namib means "an area where there is nothing", but to anyone who has visited this starkly beautiful ribbon of sand, that label is misleading. The Namib Desert stretches 2,000 kilometres from the Olifants River in the Cape Province of South Africa, where it merges with the Kalahari Desert on the plateau atop the Great Escarpment. The ever-shifting folds of sand, which range from yellow-grey along the Atlantic coast to brick-red inland, date back at least 55 million years, possibly longer, making the Namib the world's oldest desert. The dunes here are interspersed with dry pans, like western Namibia's spectacular Sossusvlei Dunes, which can reach more than 300 metres high and stretch for 15 to 30 kilometres. These dunes are often referred to as "star dunes", which describes their shape, the result of multidirectional winds that create fine halos of sands rising from their peaks.

The Namib is also one of the driest places on earth, and a visit to the desolate Skeleton Coast – named for the mariners who survived their shipwrecks only to die in the desert – confirms this. But even in a sparsely populated desert there is life: underground streams cross the wasteland, and the tangled Welwitschia Mirabilis, a plant with a life span of more than 1,000 years, scratches out an existence here.

Although only 12 percent of the world's deserts are sand dunes, they command a lot of attention, particularly when they're moving. If driven by strong winds, dunes may move as fast as 15 metres a year, but on average, barchan (wind-driven) dunes move only about 3 metres a year. Any attempt to control the flow of dunes is doomed to failure, as residents of the once diamond-rich town of Kolmanskop, Namibia, discovered. Between 1911 and 1914, 5 million carats (approximately 1,000 kilos) of diamonds were found here. But severe water problems and a constant sand-blasting wind drove miners to richer fields, and Kolmanskop began retreating into its current desert state. What remains above sand today is a ghostly shell of a once-glittering town.

EARTH'S LONGEST SAND DUNES

Simpson Desert
Location: Central Australia
Total Length: 200 km
Coordinates: 25° 00′ 00″ S | 137° 00′ 00″ E

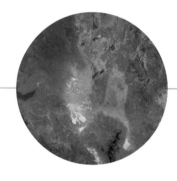

Dunes form when sand is blown into the sheltered area behind an obstacle, such as a wooded area, a collection of boulders, or even houses. The sand pile grows as more grains accumulate, with the direction and force of the wind determining its shape and size. The dunes in the 130,000-square-kilometre Simpson Desert in Australia can run for as much as 200 kilometres.

Large expanses of desert with sand ridges, scattered growth of stunted mulga trees (a type of acacia scrub), hummock grass, and dry salt lakes attract visitors to Simpson Desert Conservation Park, but the arid and broiling daytime temperatures – which are only partly offset by seasonal rains – can be unrelenting. A number of aboriginal tribes originally populated these areas, concentrated around the watercourses on the desert boundaries. Some of their wells and stone arrangements can still be found in the central desert today. European settlements appeared about 150 years ago.

The beauty of the Simpson Desert comes from its many parallel red-sand ridges. Hundreds of thousands of years ago, this basin was alternately covered by freshwater lakes or the sea. Roughly 40,000 years ago, when the centre of the Australian continent dried out, the top layers of sand became mobile and were swept into the wide Lake Eyre Basin. These winds formed the parallel longitudinal dunes, which average 20 metres high. The sand colours vary from yellowish-white (near watercourses) to red (tinted by a coating of iron oxide). Clay, salt pans, sand drifts, plains, and flats fill out this rugged landscape.

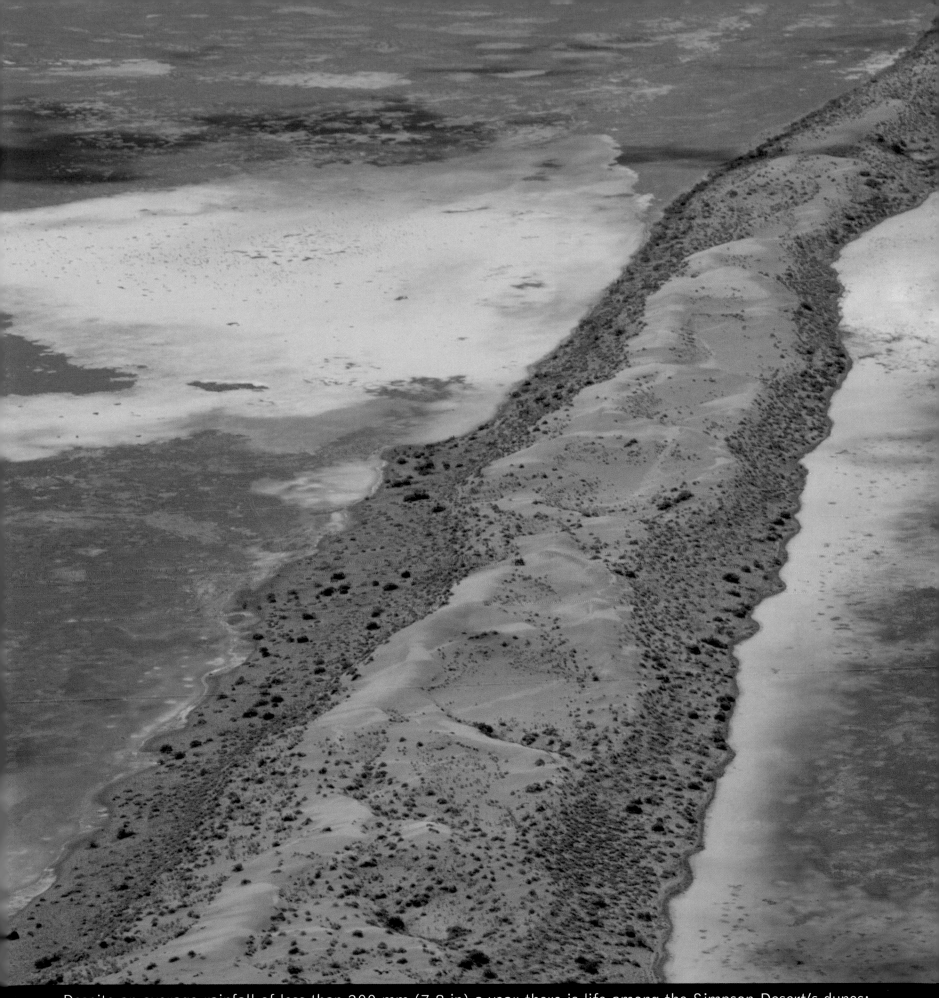

Despite an average rainfall of less than 200 mm (7.8 in) a year, there is life among the Simpson Desert's dunes: hardy spinifex and cane grass somehow flourish along the dune crests. Meanwhile Sturt's desert peas, Cunningham bird flowers, and Billy Buttons all burst into flower at the same time each year after the baptism of brief rains.

EARTH'S LARGEST DESERTS

Unless otherwise noted, measurements are correct according to the Columbia Gazetteer of the World and the Merriam Webster Geographical Dictionary. Place names verified through the United States Board on Geographic Names and the National Imagery Mapping Agency's (NIMA) geographic names database.

1 SAHARA DESERT
LOCATION: North Africa | SIZE: 9,065,000 km^2

2 AUSTRALIAN DESERT
LOCATION: Australia | SIZE: 1,371,000 km^2

3 ARABIAN DESERT
LOCATION: South-West Asia | SIZE: 2,300,000 km^2

4 GOBI DESERT
LOCATION: Central Asia | SIZE: 1,300,000 km^2

5 KALAHARI DESERT
LOCATION: South Africa | SIZE: 259,000 km^2

EARTH'S LARGEST GYPSUM DUNE

White Sands National Monument
Location: New Mexico, U.S.A.
Coordinates: 32° 36' 17" N | 106° 30' 07" W

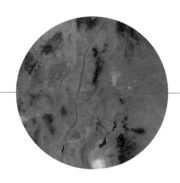

Emerging from the centre of the Tularosa Basin, a mountain-ringed valley at the northern end of the Chihuahuan Desert, is a blinding white pile of powder that rises 18 metres skyward. This reflective six-story mountain is White Sands National Monument, a 700-square-kilometre expanse of desert covered by glistening white sand that constitutes the world's largest gypsum dune field.

Gypsum (calcium sulphate) is a mineral that originates high in the San Andres and Sacramento Mountains. Over time, mountain-elevation rain and snow dissolve gypsum from the rocks and transport it to the Tularosa Basin, where it is trapped in a stew of sediment. As the water from this stew evaporates, the gypsum forms crystals, which eventually break down into grains. The wind then blows these grains into huge, white, dusty dunes. While most sand – such as the sand in much of the Sahara – is made of heavy quartz, gypsum is soft and light, making it ideal for warm-weather sledding. But like all dunes, these sands are always advancing, blanketing new terrain as they're driven forward by strong south-west winds. As the sand grains accumulate into a dune, they bounce up its gentle windward slope, rippling its surface. At the dune's steep leading edge, sand builds up until gravity pulls it down the slip face, which moves the dune forward.

Four types of dune make up White Sands: crescent-shaped barchan dunes, which form in areas with strong winds but a limited supply of sand; transverse dunes, which are long ridges of sand; parabolic dunes, which form on the dune field's edges; and dome dunes, the fastest movers, which are low mounds of sand that move up to 10 metres per year.

Gypsum is used to make plaster of Paris, a boon to sculptors and artists for many centuries. These white sands in New Mexico, shaped by the wind into the flowing ridges of a much-magnified human fingertip, show how the material can just as easily shape itself into forms that any artist would envy.

EARTH'S LARGEST SAND ISLAND

Fraser Island
Location: Queensland, Australia
Total Size: About 171 km^2
Coordinates: 25° 15' 00" S | 153° 10' 00" E

Fraser Island appeared from nowhere with the help of the winds. Formed during the Ice Age, when winds carried tremendous quantities of sand from New South Wales and deposited it along the coast of Queensland, Fraser Island would be remarkable merely for being the planet's largest sand island. But Fraser Island, or Great Sandy Island, as many people call this World Heritage site, is a combination of many distinct ecosystems. Sandy surf beaches, mangrove swamps, rain forest, coastal scrub, heath, and 40 or so lakes all can be found here. Half the world's perched freshwater dune lakes (found above the water table) are located here, as well as enormous sand dunes. Pine trees, palm trees, the rare angiopteris fern (one of the world's largest varieties), 200 species of bird, wallabies, dingoes, snakes, possums, turtles, and flying foxes all call this coastal dune system their home.

In the past, sand mining and destructive logging threatened this fragile ecosystem. But local efforts to preserve Fraser Island have succeeded in warding off the impact of harmful industrial practices.

EARTH'S MULTICOLOURED BEACHES

Hawaiian Islands, U.S.A.
Black Sand Beach at Punalu'u: 21° 35′ N | 157° 54′ W
Red Sand Beach at Hana: 20° 46′ N | 155° 59′ W
White Sand Beach on Kauai: 22° 00′ N | 159° 41′ W
Green Sand Beach near Ka Lae: 18° 54′ N | 155° 41′ W

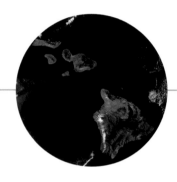

Beaches in Florida and the Caribbean are made out of crushed shells and coral. Bermuda is famous for its pink sand. But the origins of all these beaches are the same: the reefs around them supply the primary ingredients that determine their colour, and most sands are more or less monochromatic. The beaches encircling the Hawaiian Islands, however, supply a stunning contrast.

Hawaii's Big Island and other volcanically active areas are noted for their black-sand beaches. They occur when waves and currents build a beach from black grains of glass deposited by lava. The black-sand beach at Punalu'u, in the Kau district, is located at the edges of a new lava delta created by the eruption of the Puna volcano. Hawaii's longest stretch of white sand is Polihale Beach, on the island of Kauai. Like its Caribbean equivalents, this beach is composed primarily of crushed shells and coral, with a sprinkling of volcanic ash. It stretches for 27 kilometres and supports dunes as high as 30 metres. Because the beach is unprotected — it faces the ocean head-on — the surf and currents can be fierce, and the beach itself can take a pounding.

The sand on the small, secluded, crescent-shaped red-sand beach near Hana village, on the island of Maui, is almost entirely composed of finely ground red cinders that originated in an ancient cinder cone downwind from a magma-spewing vent. The beach itself is located within the caldera, the collapsed core of the cinder cone. A high cliff wall rises behind it.

The most spectacular beach is the green-sand Papakolea Beach, near the southernmost point of Hawaii, at the base of Pu'u Mahana. A rare geological phenomenon, green-sand beaches are formed by the erosion of olivine crystals from the surrounding volcanic cinder cone. As ocean waves crashed against the volcanic coast, they wore away the cone and created a small bay; waves then carried the lighter grains of volcanic-ash sand out to sea and left the denser olivine crystals behind.

This red beach is in Maui, named after a cunning demigod who fished up the island from the ocean with a magic hook.

Pu'u Mahana is a 24-metre cinder cone, open to the sea, with green olivine sand below and purple rocks above.

LARGEST CANYON IN THE WESTERN HEMISPHERE

The Grand Canyon
Location: Arizona, south-western U.S.A.
Total Size: 446 km long | average width 16 km | 1.6 km deep
Coordinates: 36° 03′ 16″ N | 112° 08′ 19″ W

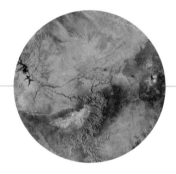

The Grand Canyon in Arizona qualifies as a rock star, and a very old one at that. Its oldest rock stratum, Vishnu Schist, dates back roughly 1.7 billion years, and the sediments themselves span 320 million years. Apart from its size, the Grand Canyon's most remarkable feature is the glimpse it offers into Earth's evolution. Its walls record ancient seas, streams, and winds in a 10-layer cake that, beginning about 6 million years ago, was excavated by a massive river now called the Colorado. As this river, which drops 670 metres over nearly 200 rapids as it roars towards the Gulf of California, cut through limestone, sandstone, and shale, it revealed not just geological clues but also biological treasures, in the form of marine invertebrate fossils (sponges, sea lilies, coral) that help explain the origins of life.

When the geologist Clarence Dutton examined the Grand Canyon between 1875 and 1881 and named many of its features, he was taken aback by the abundance and variety of rock formations, particularly buttes. "Any one [of these buttes], if it could be placed by itself upon some distant plain, would be regarded as one of the great wonders of the world. Yet here they crowd each other ... the power and grandeur is quite beyond description."

The Grand Canyon was first settled 3,000 years ago by the Anasazi Indians. John Wesley Powell, a one-armed Civil War veteran, led the first documented descent of the Colorado River in 1869, and he described the canyon's walls as "portals of the infernal region". In 1903, Theodore Roosevelt declared it the one natural phenomenon every American should see, and today, this colossal rent in the northern Arizona landscape is a World Heritage site that draws 5 million visitors a year. From timeworn vantage points atop the Kaibab limestone cliffs, these visitors are washed in a golden glow reflected from iron oxides in the canyon's sediment, yet another of its unforgettable features.

This valley of slick rock is at Paria National Park, about 40 km from the Grand Canyon. The sandstone runs through

a striking palette of earth tones, laid down by rivers, twisted by geological stress, and polished by glaciers.

EARTH'S LARGEST CANYON AND DEEPEST GORGE

Great Canyon of Yarlung and Namcha Barwa Gorge
Location: Tibetan Himalaya
Total Size: 496 km long | 5.3 km deep
Namcha Barwa Coordinates: 29° 40′ 00″ N | 95° 10′ 00″ E

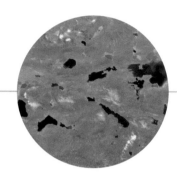

Arizona's Grand Canyon is not the world's largest canyon any more. In 1994, the American Geography Committee recognized the Great Canyon of the Yarlung Zangbo (Brahmaputra) River in the Himalaya as the grandest of all canyons on Earth. The dimensions confirm its standing: it is 50 kilometres longer than its North American counterpart and more than 4,000 metres deeper. The deepest portion of the Great Canyon is believed to be the Namcha Barwa Gorge, which was discovered and documented by members of an American expedition of scientists on October 8, 1993. Before this discovery, Earth's deepest gorge was declared to be Peru's Colca River Canyon, which sinks to 3.2 kilometres and was first descended by a group of Polish explorers in 1981.

The Great Canyon of Yarlung stretches from Tibet to Bangladesh and was created 55 million years ago when tectonic forces caused the Eurasian plate to crash into the Indian plate, giving rise to the Himalaya and the Plateau of Tibet. The region covered by the canyon ranges from snowy mountains and glaciers to tropical rain forests, and it supports wildlife, including tigers, leopards, red pandas, and bears. Gorges – deep, narrow valleys with nearly vertical sides – frequently form in areas where the land has been uplifted, where glaciers cut through deep valleys, or where streams have carved channels through rock that is relatively resistant to weathering. Hiking into the gorges poses numerous dangers (flash flooding among them), which is why some of Earth's deepest trenches remain undiscovered.

'Rocks crumble, make new forms,
oceans move the continents,
mountains rise up and down like ghosts
yet all is natural, all is change.'

Anne Sexton

Named after the Hindu goddess of destruction, the Kali Gandaki gorge in the Great Canyon plunges a vertiginous 6,660 m at Tatopani to the River Kali Gandaki. It slices its way between two towering massifs, Dhaulagiri (8,172 m) and Annapurna (8,091 m). For millennia, the gorge formed a vital trading link between India and remote Tibet

EARTH'S DEEPEST CAVE

Gouffre Mirolda
Location: Haute Savoie region, France
Total Size: Estimated length, 10,000 m | measured depth, 1,733 m
Coordinates: 46° 00′ 00″ N | 06° 20′ 00″ E

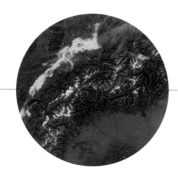

The title of Earth's deepest cave seems to stand for only a short time, as the deepest depths keep growing deeper, though none truly dents the globe's surface.

At the time of this book's publication, the deepest cave on Earth was determined to be Gouffre Mirolda, in the Haute Savoie region of France. For years, Lamprechtsofen-Vogelschacht in Salzburg, Austria, was accepted as the world's deepest cave. With depths of 1,632 metres, this winding, twisting underground maze offered more than enough subterrain for even the fastest-moving cavern aficionados. And then in 2001, a Ukrainian/Russian scientific team re-explored Georgia's Veronja Cave, located in the Arabica massif of the Caucasus Mountains, and determined its depth to be 1,710 metres, temporarily earning it the title of Earth's deepest cave, before Gouffre Mirolda took it away. Future explorations of Veronja and Lamprechtsofen could enable these one-time record holders to regain their former glory.

Deep caves are discovered all the time. In 1986, cavers not far from Carlsbad Caverns National Park in New Mexico reached the bottom of a well-known 27-metre pit called Misery Hole, only to uncover the Lechuguilla cave beneath it. So far, 157 kilometres of this "new" cave system have been mapped, and with a depth of 479 metres, Lechuguilla is currently the deepest limestone cave in the United States.

Burrowing deeper into the earth with lamp and harness, cavers are obsessed with plumbing the deepest hole of all. This photo was taken at Lechuguilla in the south-western U.S. state of New Mexico. It may seem shallow compared with its French, Austrian and Caucasian rivals, but caves have a habit of opening into unsuspected new depths.

EARTH'S LARGEST CAVE CHAMBER

Sarawak Chamber
Location: Sarawak, Malaysia
Total Size: Approximate length, 700 m | width, 451 m | average height, 100 m
Coordinates: 04°04' 00" N | 114° 56' 00" E

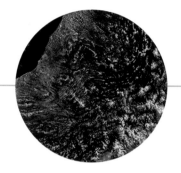

Each cave is like a fascinating hidden theatre with its own decoration, shape, personality, acoustics, and smell. It's even more dramatic than a theatre because it's difficult to get into: you have to scrape your way through limestone, marble, dolomite, or lava tubes to arrive at a perfectly dark, dripping gallery. But the journey is worth the hardship to enthusiasts, particularly those who travel to Gunung Mulu National Park, on the island of Borneo in northern Sarawak, Malaysia. This park is named for Gunung Mulu, a peak 2,377 metres high that is said to be the most cavernous mountain in the world. At least 290 kilometres of explored caves constitute a vast subterranean network that keeps spelunkers swooning.

The crown jewel in this underworld is the Lubang Nasib Bagus (meaning "good luck cave"), which contains the Sarawak chamber, a chamber large enough to accommodate a gothic cathedral with room to spare. The huge tropical river caves in the Gunung Mulu National Park are the result of both the geological uplift in the soft limestone soil some 2 million to 5 million years ago and the erosion of the rock by rivers. The Sarawak chamber contains sediment deposits and oval flood tubes that link the different cave levels.

Along with the Sarawak chamber, the Gunung Mulu National Park contains another Earth extreme: Deer Cave (Gua Payau) is the world's largest natural cave passage, measuring 120 to 150 metres in diameter.

EARTH'S LONGEST CAVE SYSTEM

Mammoth Cave
Location: Kentucky, central U.S.A.
Total Size: At least 566 km in area
Coordinates: 37° 11′ 10″ N | 86° 06′ 00″ W

Middle Earth is no doubt what a nameless explorer was looking for 2,000 years ago when a boulder pinned him to a ledge of a cave and he was entombed forever beneath the earth's surface. In 1935, two Mammoth Cave guides happened to discover this well-preserved body, which belonged to a group of people that archaeologists refer to as "Early Woodland", who hunted game and gathered wild plants in the eastern woodland forests.

Mammoth Cave is the world's longest cave system, worming its way beneath the hills and forests of south-central Kentucky. The exact length of the Mammoth Cave and Flint Ridge Cave System is not known, but multilevel, subterranean passages extending at least 566 kilometres have been explored and mapped since 1799. The extent of this massive system initially was of little concern to explorers; rather, the mineral they were made of, saltpetre, a key ingredient in gunpowder, was the big draw. But over time, the actual length

of Mammoth Cave became a tantalizing question for cave aficionados.

Rugged hills, high rocky bluffs, and two major rivers define the sloping surface area of Mammoth Cave National Park. Numerous deep cracks, valleys, and underground streams cut into the porous layers of limestone rock underlying this region. For more than 25 million years, a relentless flow of water containing carbonic acid ate away at rock layers to form sinkholes and caves, hollowing out long passageways. Seeping groundwater created huge vertical shafts, called pits and domes.

Various limestone formations, including huge chambers, stalagmites, stalactites, and gypsum flowers, as well as subterranean lakes and rivers (with names like Pillars of Hercules and Frozen Niagara), are the home of animals that have adapted to the dark environment. These include cave crickets, blind beetles and bats, eyeless fish, and eyeless crayfish.

'And in its empty course we glide today,
Glancing like fireflies with the lantern's gleam,
Strange visitants, to vanish by and by,
As the lost, nameless river passed away.'

Julia Dinsmore, *Mammoth Cave*

EARTH'S LONGEST, DEEPEST, NARROWEST SLOT CANYON

Buckskin Gulch
Location: Utah-Arizona border, U.S.A.
Total Size: 21.6 km long | 244 m deep in places
Coordinates: 37° 00′ 48″ N | 111° 59′ 58″ W

Most canyons have the familiar "V" shape, with a river running through the middle. But a slot canyon is much narrower, with nearly vertical sides, a canyon in which you can touch both walls at the same time. Buckskin Gulch, in the Paria Canyon of the Vermillion Cliffs Wilderness Area in Utah, is the world's longest, deepest, narrowest slot canyon. The canyon is the same width at the top as at the bottom, an average of 3 metres wide, but some passages are so narrow that a human body can barely squeeze through. The deepest areas are always dark. A sign hanging near an entrance to Buckskin Gulch warns hikers: "Flash Floods Can Occur at Any Time of the Year ... the Emergency Response Is Never Rapid."

Geologists believe that this area was once a huge sand-dune desert compacted millions of years ago by wind and rain in the red rock known as Navajo sandstone. Flash floods carved up the stone, creating sculptural, undulating canyon walls. A spooky menagerie of rattlesnakes, tarantulas, wrens, and rock squirrels make their home here, and pools of water collect in some areas. More pleasant surprises are the Anasazi petroglyphs etched into the walls. A lone warrior waving his bow and cliff-scrambling bighorn sheep decorate this sheer, red, deeply desolate landform.

EARTH'S LARGEST CRATER

Sudbury Crater
Location: Ontario, south-eastern Canada
Total Size: 140 km wide
Coordinates: 46° 30′ 00″ N | 80° 58′ 00″ W

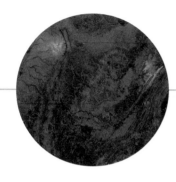

For decades, scientists have debated whether Sudbury Crater was created by a meteorite or whether it is a collapsed volcano. But no one has ever doubted that this elongated, bowl-shaped depression in Ontario, Canada, is the world's largest crater. The crater itself, which is estimated to be nearly 2 billion years old, continues to raise questions not just about its own origins but also about the earth's own evolution.

The Sudbury district is also the home of one of the world's largest and richest nickel-copper sulphide deposits. When Sudbury was first explored, geologists surmised that this ore rose from the earth's mantle as a mass of red-hot magma that solidified before breaking through the surface. But later they discovered that the composition of Sudbury's ore belied this initial supposition. Scientists now believe that an object from outer space, about the size of Mount Everest, created this giant impact crater and left behind unique carbon material in the form of hollow, soccer-ball-shaped molecules with helium trapped inside that provided the necessary organic material to create life on Earth. This could be called the "star dust" theory of evolution.

To give you an idea of the impact of such a cosmic bomb crashing at full speed into solid rock, imagine this: if such an object were to fall to Earth today, it would destroy everything (forests, towns, people) within 800 kilometres of its impact site. The intense heat generated by the impact would cause at least several thousand cubic kilometres of volcanic gas, sulphur, CO, and CO_2-rich, oxygen-poor air surrounding the contact zone to ignite, and the explosion would be felt across North America. Finally, with the atmosphere loaded with particles and dust, a dark, cold winter would set in.

EARTH'S LARGEST VOLCANIC CRATER

Toba
Location: Northern Sumatra, Indonesia
Total Size: 1,160 km²
Coordinates: 02° 35′ 00″ N | 98° 50′ 00″ E

Indonesia's largest lake (also the largest lake in South-east Asia), Danau Toba, occupies an ancient caldera, or a collapsed volcanic cone, hollowed out by a tremendous explosion and filled with water over thousands of years. The volcano last erupted around 70,000 years ago, and the hole it left behind is the earth's largest known inactive, flooded volcanic crater.

Located in the volcanic Barisan mountain range, which cuts a diagonal swath across the Island of Sumatra, Danau Toba (following page), is 910 metres above sea level. Its coast is fringed with precipitous cliffs that drop hundreds of feet into the aquamarine waters, rocky ledges that round out the vast and lushly vegetated area of the caldera.

One beautiful result of the area's volcanic activity was the rise of Samosir island in the middle of Lake Toba. About the size of Singapore, Samosir is surrounded by green cliffs leading up to the central highlands, which are covered with rice paddies and palm trees.

Dutch writer Louis Couperus fell in love with the crater lake, which he described in his 1923 travel journal, *Eastward*: "It was the incredible beauty of an ancient, volcanic world, which through her cataclysms stayed a paradise of giants and gods. There is something gigantic in this nature and herein lies Lake Toba as a blue jewel, luminescent between the pearl-white, straight rocks."

'A blue jewel, luminescent between the pearl-white, straight rocks.'

Local legend tells of a man living in Danau Toba who caught a fish in his trap, which miraculously turned into a beautiful princess. She agreed to marry him, as long as he promised to never say anything of her origins.

Years later, scolding their child for eating his midday meal, he lost his temper and exclaimed, 'You damned daughter of a fish!' and thus unleashed an earthquake.

EARTH'S LARGEST VOLCANIC CALDERAS

1 DANAU TOBA, SUMATRA, INDONESIA | 100 x 30 km
2 YELLOWSTONE CALDERA, WYOMING, U.S.A | 85 x 45 km
3 TAUPO, NORTH ISLAND, NEW ZEALAND | 32 x 25 km
4 LONG VALLEY, CALIFORNIA, U.S.A | 32 x 17 km

Information provided by the United States Geological Survey

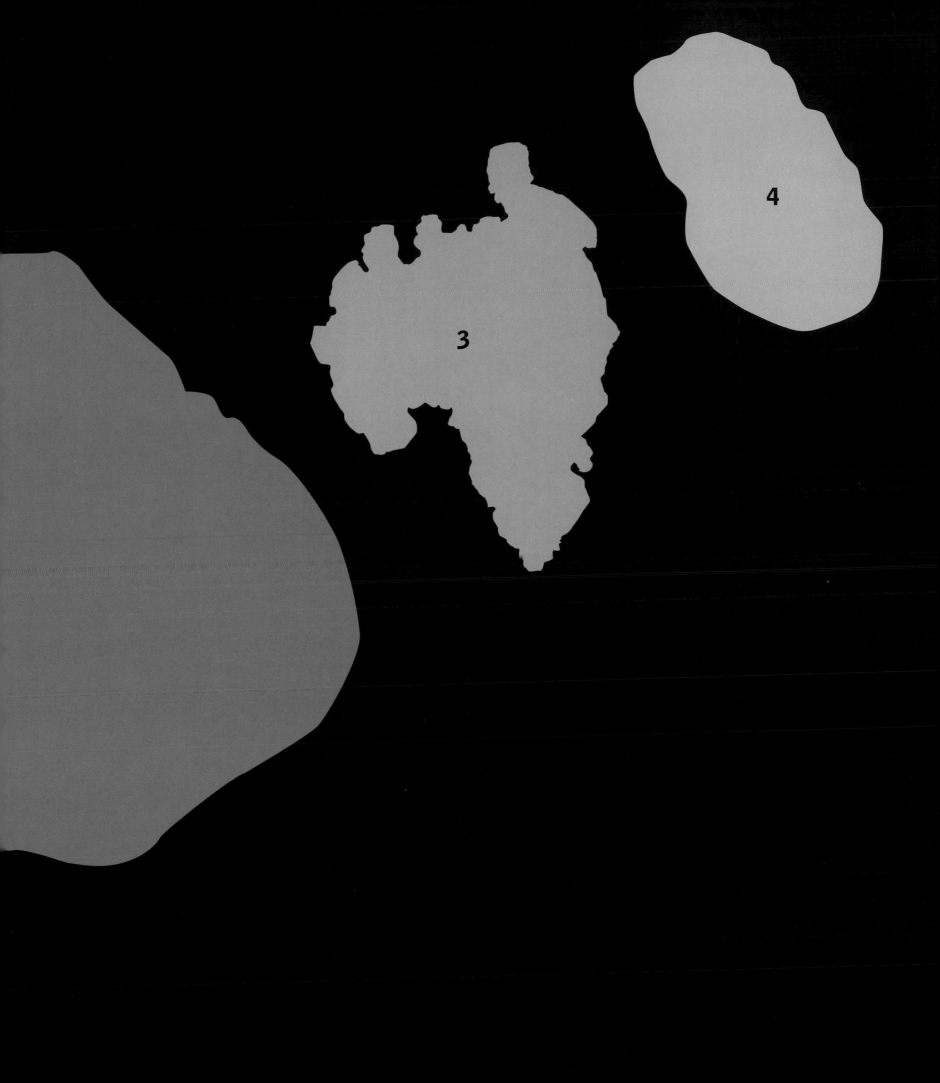

EARTH'S LARGEST ISLAND

Greenland
Location: North America and the Arctic Circle
Total Size: 2,166,086 km²
Coordinates: 72° 00′ 00″ N | 40° 00′ 00″ W

Kalaallit Nunaat ("land of the people"), as the locals call Greenland, is harsh, forbidding, and almost completely buried beneath a permanent cap of ice and snow. More than twice the size of the world's second-largest island, New Guinea, Greenland's rugged coastline, which is deeply indented by fjords and inlets, is nearly equal to the earth's circumference at the equator. Greenland's northernmost point is less than 800 kilometres from the North Pole. Its ice sheet constitutes roughly 10 percent of all the world's ice; it averages 1,500 metres in thickness, reaching 4,270 metres in some places. Each year, Greenland's glaciers calve an estimated 10,000 to 15,000 icebergs.

Greenland has only 56,076 inhabitants, most of whom live along the western coast, but this icy landscape has loomed large in the mythologies of cultures curious about life in the world's northern reaches. The first Palaeo-Eskimo settlers likely arrived 5,000 years ago via Canada, and while each successive culture left its mark, it was the Thule culture that invented the kayak, harpoon, and dogsled, which still are used today. The island began to be colonized in 985 C.E., when Eric the Red, a Norseman, named it Greenland in order to attract potential settlers. Norse sagas recount in detail the history of Greenland's settlement, but what Greenlanders especially love about their island, and the images that tourists take away, are the long, sinuous fjords, expansive glaciers, blue icebergs, and the white sun, low on the horizon, emitting very little heat but casting a haze over the Arctic terrain. Long, dark winters in high latitudes sometimes cause depression – which the Inuit call *perlerorneq*, or "the burden".

EARTH'S FASTEST-GROWING ISLAND

Iceland
Location: North Atlantic Ocean
Coordinates: 65° 00′ 00″ N | 18° 00′ 00″ W

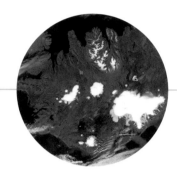

Iceland is the geographic teenager of all the earth's islands, growing constantly but fitfully in spurts. The island is a young basalt plateau that straddles the Mid-Atlantic Ridge, a dynamic seam where two of Earth's plates are slowly, and often explosively, pulling apart. Over the course of an average human's lifetime, Iceland will grow about a car's length.

Underground hot springs abound in Iceland (their steam is used to heat houses), and its celebrated geysers are testament to the fiery forces working beneath this chilly Arctic landscape. About 200 volcanoes, many of them still active, rise over Iceland. The highest is 1,490-metre Mount Hekla, but a more famous volcanic feature looms off the southern coast.

Surtsey is a volcanic island measuring 3 square kilometres that appeared unexpectedly from beneath the churning waters of the North Atlantic. In November 1963, a bubbling volcano broke through the waves, emitting explosions of ash, cinders, and pumice in a column shooting more than 305 metres high. Lava spewed out of the water from 1964 through 1967; this new magma cooled to heal the fissure and form new ocean crust underwater. Then the magma created a shell over the ash above the water to harden the young volcano into an island. The hot spot beneath Iceland is so active that one-third of all the lava to surface on earth in the last 1,000 years is of Icelandic origin. Locals named this gusher Surtsey after Surtur, the ancient Norse god who was appointed to set fire to Earth on the day the gods are dethroned, a fitting name for a land that breathes fire from beneath its icy shell.

Rapid territorial growth is the result of frequent volcanic eruptions. Hekla is both the largest and most active, and Icelanders have been counting its upheavals for 900 years: at least 15 major eruptions from a total of 167 since 1104.

EARTH'S GREATEST RAIN FOREST

Amazon Basin
Location: Brazil, South America
Total Size: 7,050,000 km²
Coordinates: 02° 30' 00" S | 60° 00' 00" W

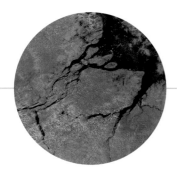

Containing more than half the earth's remaining rain forest and covering one-third of the South American continent, the Amazon basin holds the world's largest reserve of biological resources. When people refer to this vast stretch of land as a "green paradise", they're not exaggerating. Although most of this luxuriant rain forest is still pristine wilderness, in the last 30 years, government-sponsored road-building projects, colonization schemes, and industrial developments have transformed large tracts of green forest into polluted factory sites and sprawling settlements.

Through the Amazon basin runs the world's largest river by volume, the 6,436-kilometre Amazon. Of the 22,767 species of plants known in the world, 16,619 (almost three-fourths) can be found here. Whereas only 150 kinds of fish exist in Europe, at least 1,500 species live in the Amazon's waters. In addition, an immense variety of insects, birds, reptiles, and mammals consider Amazonia home. The forests provide rubber, hardwoods, Brazil nuts, diamonds, gold, petroleum, key ingredients for modern medicines, and more. Yet for all its strength, the Amazon basin remains a fragile and increasingly endangered ecosystem, one subject to aggressive deforestation and ecological plunder.

Now that tropical rain forests are being laid to waste with such haste, it's sobering to recall that less than 50 years ago their destruction was far less advanced. In his classic 1958 study of the forest Indians living in the northern Amazon tributaries of Guyana, botanist Nicholas Guppy wrote: 'Forests so completely virgin were almost unique upon earth, and

it was important that they should be studied while they were still undisturbed – especially as they were likely to be extremely ancient in type.' And he added: 'All these forests, uniform-seeming yet infinitely varied, were like works of art ... their beauty that of the close approach of all these interacting qualities to a point of rest, or equilibrium.'

EARTH'S DRIEST PLACE

Atacama Desert
Location: Chile
Total Size: 140,000 km²
Coordinates: 24° 30′ 00″ S | 69° 15′ 00″ W

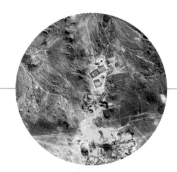

The bone-dry Atacama Desert could be termed "vegetatively challenged". Only a few thousand people sustain themselves by farming here, and they all tend crops near salt marshes or rivers. Salt basins, sand, and lava rock form the cool, coastal Atacama Desert in northern Chile, extending south from the border of Peru. Rainfall here is barely measurable, averaging less than 0.01 centimetres annually; some years pass without a drop. Some places in Atacama haven't seen rain for more than 400 years.

The Atacama is small, only a tiny fraction of the Sahara's size and roughly equivalent to North America's Mojave Desert. It rises 610 metres above sea level; its average daily temperatures range from freezing to 21°C; and the tiny amount of precipitation it receives comes from fog that blows in from the ocean. The few plants able to survive there either live on the combined moisture from fog and dew or sink long taproots deep into the earth to gather water from below. Flamingos feed on the red algae that grows in the briny waters of Atacama's salt lakes.

Human communities have endured in this forbidding landscape for thousands of years (desert dwellers harvest water using fog catchers, giant screens that catch fog and conduct water into cisterns), and some of the most ancient mummies (20,000 years old) have been uncovered here. Some visitors imagine this landscape must be like Mars.

EARTH'S LONGEST RIFT

Great Rift Valley
Location: North-eastern Africa
Total Size: 6,400 km long
Coordinates: **Jordan** 31° 00′ 00″ N | 36° 00′ 00″ E
Beira, Mozambique 19° 50′ 37″ S | 34° 50′ 20″ E

If scientists are correct, the Great Rift Valley – an immense series of cracks stretching from Jordan to the coast of Mozambique – is the beginning of a fault zone that could one day split Africa in two, creating a new ocean. It is an extension of the Mid-Oceanic Ridge system, most of which is submerged, and is, on average, 48 to 64 kilometres wide.

From far above, the Great Rift Valley looks like a huge scar through the eastern half of Africa and the Middle East. Patches of extinct or inactive volcanoes and tectonic lakes are found along this enormous depression, which was created when the tectonic separation of plates split the earth's crust and parallel fault lines sank to become narrow valleys. If these rifts continue to form, in several million years eastern Africa could float away and become an island (much like Madagascar).

Among the Great Rift Valley's prominent features is the Jordan fault zone, which gave rise to the Hula Valley, Lake Tiberias, and the Dead Sea. Deep canyons and incised wadis (dry stream valleys) define the eastern and western escarpments of the Jordan Rift Valley. The Danakil Depression in Ethiopia descends 116 metres below sea level, contains large salt lakes, and is among Earth's hottest places, with temperatures exceeding 49°C.

Rift valleys and fault zones abound on the earth's surface. California's 1,200-km-long San Andreas Fault (above), marks the boundary between two plates and causes about 10,000 (mostly small) earthquakes each year. This fault

system runs almost the entire length of California and is, in some spots, as much as 16 km deep. The land moves across the San Andreas Fault at a rate of 56 mm a year.

EARTH'S LARGEST UNBROKEN, UNFLOODED CALDERA

Ngorongoro Caldera
Location: Tanzania, Africa
Total Size: 264 km²
Coordinates: 03° 10′ 00″ S | 35° 35′ 00″ E

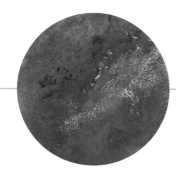

Travellers to the Ngorongoro Conservation Area – often called the "Garden of Eden" for its spectacular concentration of wildlife – are usually fixated on spotting the "big five" (lion, leopard, buffalo, rhino, and elephant). But they would do well to focus on the crater itself, which is the world's largest unbroken, unflooded caldera, a deep and broad basin that formed 2.5 million years ago when a volcano exploded and collapsed inward. This verdant caldera shelters a Noah's Ark of animals within an area 22.5 kilometres across at its widest point. Near the centre of the crater is a shallow soda lake, its surface bright pink with hundreds of flamingos, its depth fed by streams running down the caldera's walls. Rain forest and brush cover the steep mountainsides that encircle

marshlands and clover pastures.

Ngorongoro lies within the Great Rift Valley and is home not just to the big five but also to hippos, gnus, cheetah, warthogs, gazelle, hyenas, and hundreds of bird species. More than 42,000 Masai live in the Ngorongoro Conservation Area, and to them, tourism is both a boon and threat. Ngorongoro is also the location of the Olduvai Gorge, where Louis and Mary Leakey discovered the remains of Zinjanthropus bosei, a distant ancestor of man believed to be 1.8 million years old. "The Cradle of Mankind", as the area is now called, is full of fossilized footprints, remains of ancient tools, and bones from now-extinct prehistoric species.

The Serengeti National Park contains the Ngorongoro Conservation Area. Vast herds of wildebeest enter the park from December through March. The calving season starts in January, attracting hungry lions, cheetahs, and hyenas. Like the

wildebeest they go to water, and the ever-present problem of thirst poses new dangers for mother and calf alike. The Masai, who have grazed cattle on this plain for millennia, call it *siringitu,* 'the place where the land moves on forever'.

EARTH'S LARGEST WILDLIFE REFUGE

Serengeti Plain: Home to Tanzania's Serengeti National Park, Ngorongoro Conservation Area, Maswa Game Reserve, and Kenya's Masai Mara Game Reserve
Location: Tanzania and Kenya, East Africa
Coordinates: 02° 50' 00" S | 35° 00' 00" E

The Serengeti Plain is a vast natural ecosystem in East Africa where a million wildebeest, lions, gazelle, leopards, zebras, hyenas, elephants, cheetahs, rhinoceroses, and giraffes migrate in waves across the grasslands. This 31,000-square-kilometre range, a vast savannah covered in grassy meadows strewn with trees and shrubs, is perhaps the most beautiful in all of Africa. The Serengeti Plain stretches to Lake Victoria in the west, to the soda lakes of the Great Rift Valley in the east, and to the depths of the Ngorongoro Crater in the south. The rhythm of life here is dependent on the seasonal rains. Every June, the dry season forces the world's most spectacular migration, when the herds move from the western Serengeti to the northern rivers. When the rains resume, the animals push to the south-east to calve before heading west to begin the cycle anew. The land itself changes over the year from vibrant greens to dusty browns.

The Serengeti's name comes from *siringitu*, which means "the place where the land moves on forever" in Masai. About 3 million large animals inhabit this area, which is roughly the size of Northern Ireland. It's a beautiful place, but not an easy one to live in. Plants must endure scorching dry spells, and animals must contend with clouds of insects. The ecosystem is one of the oldest on Earth. This "cradle of humanity" contains much evidence of humankind's earliest evolutionary steps. With careful conservation efforts already set in motion, Africa's Eden can be preserved.

George and Joy Adamson worked in the Serengeti to release lions into the wild. Their story was told in books and films, notably *Born Free*. But it's not only the land or the threat of predators in Africa that can be unforgiving. Joy was killed by an ex-employee in 1980, George was shot by poachers in 1989.

EARTH'S LARGEST EARTHQUAKE

Valdivia, May 22, 1960
Location: Off the southern coast of Chile
Magnitude: 9.5
Coordinates: 39° 48′ 00″ S | 73° 14′ 00″ W

Each year the earth endures more than half a million detectable earthquakes. Of these, 100,000 can be felt by people and 100 damage property and take lives.

The seismic waves and vibrations of a ground-shaking earthquake are caused by the release of energy when the underlying rock (typically near faults, or fractures, in the earth's crust) breaks or shifts under stress; this movement typically occurs at depths of less than 80 kilometres from the earth's surface. Most earthquakes occur along the boundaries of interacting oceanic and continental plates in a world-shaping process called plate tectonics. These plate boundaries also are responsible for fault zones, rifts, and volcanoes.

The seismic waves from an earthquake pass swiftly outward in all directions, much like the ripples emanating from a pebble dropped into a pond. Although an earthquake's intensity varies depending on its location, its magnitude is a constant measure of its size.

As early as 350 B.C.E., the Greek scholar Aristotle was studying earthquakes. While history's largest earthquake may never be known, the largest on record struck Chile on May 22, 1960. Measuring 9.5 on the magnitude moment scale, this earthquake's epicentre was 60 metres below the Pacific Ocean floor, 160 kilometres off the coast of Chile. The nearby towns of Valdivia and Puerto Montt were flattened, and more than 2,000 people were killed in Chile, Hawaii, Japan, and the Philippines from both the earthquake and the tsunami it created. All in all, it was more powerful than the world's largest nuclear-bomb test.

The second-largest earthquake of the 20th century struck Prince William Sound, Alaska, on Good Friday, March 28, 1964. This earthquake, measuring 9.2 on the magnitude moment scale, lasted for three minutes – an enormous amount of time, as most quakes last for less than a minute – killed 125 people, caused landslides and a tsunami that crashed against Hawaii, and is said to have moved the city of Anchorage, Alaska, 1 metre to the south. Alaska is a site of constant earth splitting, with an average of 5,000 quakes each year measuring at least M 3.5. Indeed, three of the world's 10 worst earthquakes on record were located here.

EARTH'S DEADLIEST EARTHQUAKES

July 28, 1976
Location: Tianjin, China
Magnitude: 7.8
Coordinates: 39° 08' 32" N | 117° 10' 36" E

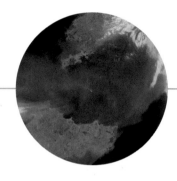

Magnitude is a relatively straightforward measurement of an earthquake's intensity. The devastation wrought by an earthquake – the cost in lives lost and property damaged – is harder to measure. Such destruction is a reflection of not only an earthquake's magnitude but also its epicentre's location, the structure of the underlying rock, the construction of local buildings, and the density of the affected population.

When a 7.8-magnitude quake struck the sleeping city of Tianjin, China, at 3.42am on July 28, 1976, its tremendous force was without question. At least one-quarter of the 1 million people of Tianjin, an industrial and mining centre 160 kilometres east of Beijing, were annihilated. The official casualty figure released by the Chinese government was 255,000, but unofficial estimates put the death toll as high as 655,000. And this was merely China's worst 20th century earthquake. On January 23, 1556, a massive tremor struck Shansi (Huaxian), in a region where at that time most people lived in caves carved from soft rock. These dwellings collapsed, killing some 830,000 people. An even more murderous quake swept under Upper Egypt (Syria) on July 5, 1201, wiping out an estimated 1.1 million people.

'We learn geology the morning after the earthquake, on ghastly diagrams of cloven mountains, upheaved plains, and the dry bed of the sea.'

Ralph Waldo Emerson

Yalova, on the south-eastern shores of the Sea of Marmara in Turkey, has always been a nice getaway from the noise of Istanbul. That was the case until August 17, 1999 at 3.02am, when a 7.2-magnitude quake hit this seismically sensitive area and killed 9,000 of the town's 60,000 residents.

EARTH'S GREATEST CONTINENTAL COLLISION

Hindu Kush
Location: Central Asia
Coordinates: 35° 00' 00" N | 71° 00' 00" E

The name Hindu Kush – Afghanistan's primary mountain range – translates as "Hindu killer". The name couldn't be more appropriate for a mountain range that lies near the boundary of the Eurasian and Indo-Australian tectonic plates, a zone where the greatest continental collision is taking place.

These glaciated, barren peaks in the eastern part of Afghanistan reach elevations of more than 7,000 metres across some 950 kilometres, forming a water divide between the Indus River Valley to the south-east and the Amu Darya River Valley to the north-west. The Hindu Kush is the westernmost extension of the Pamir Mountains, the Karakorum Mountains, and the Himalaya. Earthquakes are common here – at least four powerful quakes occur annually. This seismic activity is the result of the Indian continent's northward shift: as it moves, it collides with the Eurasian continent, causing an uplift of the Himalayan mountains and the Tibetan plateau.

The two plates are converging at about 4.4 centimetres a year, enough of an impact to raise the mighty Himalaya about 5 millimetres.

Historically, the Hindu Kush has been the site of great military moments. Its dangerous high-elevation passes were crossed by Alexander the Great, Genghis Khan, and Timur and Babur in their invasions of India. The same routes that were once strategically significant in warfare became an invaluable network for the transit of caravans. Trade routes continue today along these ancient paths. In the past, Pakistan's Khyber Pass was the key route, but the most important mountain pass now is the Kotal-e Salang, which links Kabul and points south to northern Afghanistan. This route was crucially important in recent military conflicts, evidenced by the many potholed roads and bombed-out bridges. Between a treacherous landscape and the region's precipitous politics, the Hindu Kush still lives up to its name.

Sebastian Junger

HINDU KUSH

There's something about the scale of humans in the universe that you can't understand until you've been to places in which you could never survive, or until you're standing on a mountain in a place like the Hindu Kush in Afghanistan. I was there in 2000, with the Northern Alliance, and again in the autumn of 2001, when the Northern Alliance took Kabul. This is a grand landscape, the most geographically out-there place I've ever been. We initially went out in an old Soviet helicopter, flying over endless miles of untouched mountains. If you got dropped there, you'd never find your way out. On top of this, the area was politically and militarily isolated because of the war with the Taliban. We were really in the middle of nowhere – just these rocky, rugged, bare mountains, looking much as I would imagine the mountains in Alaska to be. Not quite the pine forests of the Alps, but very jagged, spectacular peaks with a beautiful river rushing down the Panjsher Valley and out into the Somali Plains.

In a natural place of breathtaking beauty, the immensity of time and space makes you feel puny. By forgetting that we're insignificant ants on the planet, human beings are losing an ancient relationship with the universe and with the earth. Deeply ingrained in our psyche, however, is still some awareness of our vulnerability. We evolved with a concept of our smallness; we didn't evolve with an illusion of being omnipotent. If we had, we would have found ourselves in some deep trouble, and nature would have obliterated us in no time.

You feel this much more in the mountains of Afghanistan than walking the caverns of Fifth Avenue. In civilization you have the illusion that the world works on a human scale, but it doesn't. The universe is 2.5 billion years old—how old are we?

EARTH'S LARGEST LANDSLIDE

Mount St. Helens
Location: Cascade Range, south-western Washington, U.S.A.
Coordinates: 45° 55′ 43″ N | 122° 22′ 44″ W

Dormant since 1857, its snowcapped peak an image of tranquil beauty, Mount St. Helens was a beloved member of the U.S. Cascade Range. Hikers in the area knew well – or thought they did – the 2,950-metre peak.

But then, with an enormous eruption of steam on March 27, 1980, the mountain began to fall apart. Magma rose up from Mount St. Helens' cone, and fissures ruptured its sides. On May 18, 1980, a 5.1-magnitude earthquake triggered a landslide on the mountain's north face. The slope fell away in an avalanche that was followed by a lateral blast, which shot a cloud of superhot ash, stone, and poison gas more than 20 kilometres from the summit. Mudflows, pyroclastic flows, and floods came down, burying the river valleys east of the mountain in debris as far as 27 kilometres away.

The world's largest recorded landslide released 2.8 billion cubic metres of rock and mud, destroying more than 259 square kilometres of forests, killing elk, deer, bears, and coyotes, as well as five to 10 people (the first eruption and landslide together killed 66 people). A second eruption occurred a week later, on May 25, and a third followed almost a year later. In the end, Mount St. Helens achieved a trifecta of disasters – eruption, earthquake, and landslide – which blasted away its volcanic cone. Today, in place of its peak is a horseshoe-shaped crater with a depth of 750 metres and a rim elevation of 2,550 metres.

Mount St. Helens shortly before its earth-shattering blast in 1980. This mudflow was triggered by a minor eruption

EARTH'S EXTREME AVALANCHE ZONES

Europe: Swiss and Italian Alps
Western United States and Canada: Rocky Mountains, Cascades
South America: Andes
Asia: Himalaya
New Zealand: Southern Alps
Coordinates: Varied

Generally, an avalanche (a term that can incorporate landslides, mudflows, lahars, and volcanic mudflows, among other slides) is a large mass of snow, ice, rock, and other material that sweeps down a mountainside or over a precipice. This overwhelming flood of material is a natural, often seasonal, form of erosion that can be triggered by volcanic eruptions, earthquake tremors, human-made disturbances, or heavy rains. Destruction results both from the avalanche wind (the air pushed ahead of the mass) and the impact of the avalanche material itself.

The most common form of avalanche is a snowslide, which begins when an unstable mass of snow breaks away from a slope. As snow falls it picks up speed and volume as it rushes downhill in a furious river that can reach speeds of 300 kilometres per hour. Two basic types of snowslides are the less destructive "loose snow" variety, which behaves like loose sand, and the more destructive "slab avalanche", a heavy plate of snow that breaks away from a weaker underlying layer. The slab, which may be more than 10 metres thick, may bring down as much as 100 times more snow as it gathers speed. These are the true killer avalanches.

Hundreds of thousands of such avalanches occur each year in the mountains of Switzerland, Italy, the Himalaya, Japan, New Zealand, Canada, and the western United States. Famous historic avalanches include those that beset Hannibal, the Carthaginian general, and his troops as they crossed the Italian Alps to conquer Rome in 218 B.C.E. It killed about 18,000 soldiers, 2,000 horses, and many elephants. The biggest avalanche on record occurred in 1962 in Peru. The Huascarán avalanche, triggered by an earthquake, sent some 50 million cubic metres of ice, rock, glacial debris, and water speeding down an Andean mountain in about three minutes, leaving around 18,000 people dead.

The Swiss Alps have the world's largest number of avalanche fatalities: 100 each year. Most victims are buried just a few feet below the snow's surface, but escaping is nearly impossible because the snow is so compacted by its fall. One-fifth die immediately; the others must be extracted within an hour if they are to survive. If found within 15 minutes (the typical duration of air supply), a victim has a 92 percent chance of survival. But this falls to only 30 percent after 35 minutes.

Every conceivable technological rescue technique has been tried, but dogs are still the most successful searchers.

EARTH'S LARGEST NATURAL BRIDGE

Rainbow Bridge
Location: Lake Powell, Utah, U.S.A.
Total Size: 82.3 m long | 13 m thick | 10 m wide
Coordinates: 37° 04′ 39″ N | 110° 57′ 49″ W

Hidden in the rugged canyons at the base of Navajo Mountain in the Colorado Plateau, Rainbow Bridge has been revered as a sacred icon by Native American tribes for hundreds of years. From its base to the tip of its arch, Rainbow Bridge rises 88.4 metres, making it the highest natural arch in the world. Composed of stratified rock, specifically Navajo sandstone, that is hundreds of millions of years old, it's easy to envision this archway as a bridge. It was formed by an ancient stream flowing into the Colorado River, which eroded some of the weaker sedimentary rock in the area, leaving the graceful arch behind.

On May 30, 1910, U.S. President William Howard Taft created Rainbow Bridge National Monument to preserve this natural treasure, which "has an appearance much like a rainbow, and which is of great scientific interest as an example of eccentric stream erosion". When Theodore Roosevelt visited the monument in 1913, he noted that a pony trail led under the archway but that his Navajo companions rode around it. "This great natural bridge, so recently 'discovered' by white men, has for ages been known to the Indians," Roosevelt wrote. "His creed bade him never pass under an arch." Recognition brought in tourists, as did the Glen Canyon Dam, which flooded the canyons of Lake Powell and made Rainbow Bridge easier to reach. Today, this archway draws some 300,000 visitors a year, much to the chagrin of Navajo people, who still conduct religious ceremonies at their sacred site.

'The Indian's creed bade him never pass under an arch.'

Theodore Roosevelt

EARTH'S MOST OTHERWORLDLY BADLANDS

Bisti Badlands
Location: New Mexico, U.S.A.
Coordinates: 36° 49' 37" N | 108° 00' 31" W

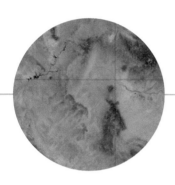

The Bisti Badlands is a rarely visited, largely unknown, surreal expanse of undulating mounds and eroded rocks. Located in the distant north-western corner of New Mexico, the Bisti/De-na-zin Wilderness is near the centre of the San Juan Basin, on the south-western Colorado Plateau. The nearest city is called Aztec, an hour's drive away. No signposts point the way from any nearby town, and no established trails lead hikers through the wilderness, which covers less than 1 square kilometre. Despite its small size, Bisti (the Navajo Indian word for "badland") is a stunning array of sedimentary rock formations; layers of sandstone, shale, silt, and coal; and chunks of petrified wood that were swept into this ancient river valley millions of years ago.

The clay hills of this labyrinthine landscape, which range in colour from sandy brown to pink to deep red, were carved by wind and rainwater erosion into fantastic shapes, tiny caves, fissures, and layered beds of sediment. Balanced rocks, hoodoos (sandstone pedestals covered by shale plates), and mushroom-shaped rocks decorate the area, appearing like signposts to another world. Over time, this erosion has also exposed dinosaur tracks and bones (of tridactyls) in the hardscrabble landscape.

Seventy million years ago Bisti was a coastal rain forest where conifers, palms, and other plants towered over the jungle floor, and dinosaurs, small reptiles, and mammals roamed. Eventually, the sea withdrew; the Rocky Mountains rose to the north and east, reversing the direction of the drainage; and sediment entombed this rain forest, petrifying plants and animals and compacting into sandstone and shale. Erosion stripped away these sedimentary deposits to reveal an ancient rain forest now frozen in stone.

EARTH'S BIGGEST MUSHROOM ROCK

Red Sea Desert
Location: Israel
Coordinates: 29° 31' 00" N | 34° 56' 00" E

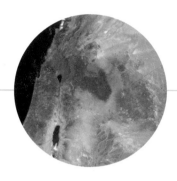

Mushroom rocks are top-heavy sandstone pedestals that tower over the eroded valley at their feet. These unique rock pillars occur along the edges of ancient seas. Over time, circulating water deposits a limy cement between sand grains, creating harder bodies of sandstone called *concretions*. Wind and water erosion blast away at these sandstone concretions, striking hard against softer sandstone that forms the stem of a mushroom rock, and more lightly at the cap. The result is an upside-down rock tower that seems to defy gravity.

How can a heavy rock cap balance on top of a narrow, eroding sandstone base? The question, it turns out, is not *how*, but *for how long*?

Mushroom rocks lead a precarious existence, and eventually, after millions of years, they fall.

The world's tallest mushroom rock (right) rises 9 metres high in the Red Sea Desert, not far from Eilat, Israel. Located in the Timna Park nature reserve, this sandstone pinnacle is a gleaming, gold-hued column in a dry desert valley of jagged escarpments and dusty ravines. Two-metre-tall limestone towers also rise in Western Australia, Arizona (south-western United States), and other places around the world. Mushroom Rock State Park in Kansas (central United States) hosts a handful of these oddities, which date back 100 million years.

You may never happen upon the Caterpillar from *Alice's Adventures in Wonderland*, perched upon a mushroom rock and puffing away on his hookah, but these strange, ancient sandstone formations do inspire curious comparisons. Animals, birds, faces, buildings, people ... one observer even reports seeing a kneeling camel.

Looking like some mute and mysterious convocation of ancient standing stones, the Pinnacles of Nambung

National Park, Western Australia, are in fact the limestone stubs of ancient fossilized trees.

EARTH'S OLDEST FOSSIL

Warrawoona Group
Location: Western Australia
Coordinates: 21° 00′ 00″ S | 119° 30′ 00″ E

When did life first appear on Earth? This is a question that keeps evolutionary scientists busy devising new kinds of measurement systems and conducting isotopic tests on ancient rock formations in order to find the world's oldest fossils. So far, these tests have led researchers to three competing theories. The first contender for oldest fossil is the Apex cherts of the Warrawoona Group in the eastern Pilbara (near Marble Bar), Western Australia, which date back 3.46 billion years. They are found in banded iron formations and are significant because they reveal the nature and antiquity of the earth's biosphere. The second contender for oldest fossil is the quartz-pyroxene rock formations in Akilia, south-west Greenland, which may contain 3.85-billion-year-old microfossils. Finally, the best evidence for the earliest life on Earth could be contained in the deep-sea sedimentary rocks from the Isua greenstone in Greenland, which is 3.7 billion to 3.8 billion years old.

The fossilized organic materials that scientists are hunting for are called stromatolites (cyanobacteria or, somewhat incorrectly, blue-green algae), which are still found today in saline lakes or hot springs but at one time were much more common. These tiny bacteria became trapped in layers of sediment, sometimes in tiny communities and often in vast, intricate branching structures that resemble modern coral. Stromatolites were around before the earth's continents formed and almost 3 billion years before the first invertebrate animals – sea pens and jellyfish – appeared. Trilobites, fish, forests, mammals, and dinosaurs followed. The earliest human ancestors appeared about 3 million years ago, but modern humans (*Homo sapiens*) didn't show up until around 100,000 years ago. In Earth's 4.5-billion-year history, humans have existed for merely a blink of an eye.

Western Australia is widely recognized as one of the world's most significant regions for studying stromatolites. Here, they are trapped in sediments on the beach in Shark Bay, Australia. They make dinosaurs look like the scaly teenagers of earth time – and now NASA is set to search for traces of these ancient crystalline creatures – on Mars.

EARTH'S STRANGEST SANDSTONE FORMATIONS

Cappadocia
Location: Turkey
Coordinates: 38° 55' 00" N | 34° 40' 00" E

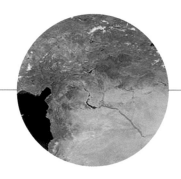

Millions of years ago, massive volcanoes on the Central Anatolian Plateau erupted, coating this area with ash and lava and creating deep valleys bordered by steep cliffs. Over millennia, the volcanic material hardened into solid rock, and ever so slowly, erosive forces of wind and water shaped these rock into cones.

The most interesting of these formations are fairy chimneys with caps; these towers have a conical-shaped body made of tufa (porous mineral rock) and volcanic ash, with a hard-rock boulder on top of it. Many types of fairy chimneys are found in Cappadocia, including mushroom-shaped towers, columns, and pointed rock islands. For more than 1,000 years, locals have hollowed out these cones, creating homes, storerooms, and churches. In the summertime, when swelteringly hot summers bake the land around these cones, the temperature inside caves remains cool.

This region has been at the heart of trade since well before the time of Julius Caesar. When Rome annexed this region in 17 C.E., horse breeding became a profitable specialty (Cappadocia means "land of pretty horses" in the ancient Hittite language). This rocky landscape also was a refuge for persecuted Christians in the 2nd century C.E., and cave churches, carved and elaborately painted by monks, are still in use.

People lived at Zelve Valley (above) until quite recently, hollowing chambers into the soft rock. There are even two sacred enclaves: the Fish and Grape churches. Elsewhere in this amazing region of central Anatolia, Turkey, at Asikli

Höyük, relics including tools and religious objects dating back to Neolithic times have been found – along with the skeleton of a woman in her early to mid-20s, showing evidence of the world's first known case of trepanning

EARTH'S MOST CALCIFIED PLACES

Mono Lake, California, U.S.A.
Coordinates: 37° 19' 36" N | 119° 01' 00" W

Mammoth Hot Springs, Yellowstone National Park, Wyoming, U.S.A.
Coordinates: 44° 46' 00" N | 110° 14' 00" W

Pamukkale (Hierapolis), Turkey
Coordinates: 37° 54' 57" N | 29° 06' 46" E

At 1 million to 3 million years old, California's Mono Lake is one of the oldest continuous lakes in North America. Although five freshwater streams feed into it, there's no drain out of it, so the dissolved salts and minerals reach high concentrations. Evaporation further increases the extreme saltiness of this lake (three times saltier than the Pacific Ocean and a thousand times more alkaline than freshwater), and the only life forms that can survive here are brine shrimp, bacteria, and alkali flies that provide food for millions of migratory waterfowl. But Mono Lake's most remarkable features are its tufa towers, unusual rock formations that cluster around its shores and beneath its surface. These towering spires and bulbous knobs are formed when underground freshwater springs laced with calcium bubble up through the lake's bottom and meet the carbonate-rich lake water. The mixture produces calcium carbonate, a white limestone sediment that collects around the mouths of the springs and grows, over time, into stunning rock towers, some more than 10 metres tall. The towers are exposed when the water level falls.

Deep beneath Mammoth Hot Springs, in Wyoming's Yellowstone National Park, magma chambers superheat groundwater so that it spurts through fissures and bubbles up. This spring water is rich in calcium carbonate, which it picks up from the sedimentary limestone that forms the region's bedrock. Once exposed to the open air, these minerals solidify. The travertine that forms the white calcium terraces gives this spectacular site the appearance of overflowing champagne flutes or tiers of vanilla-frosted cupcakes.

In a verdant valley in Turkey and nestled against high mountains along the Buyuk Menderes (Meander) River, a similar hydrological exchange produces the bone-white plateaus of Pamukkale (Hierapolis). In this white fairyland, thermal spring waters with calcium-rich salts flow over the plateau's edge, creating a fantastic formation of stalactites, cataracts, and basins.

Hierapolis, as it was known in ancient times, is dotted with Roman temples and theatres, as well as Byzantine churches and basilicas. Its modern name, Pamukkale, or 'cotton castle', rightly sets nature's achievements above those of man.

A sleeping chief, encircled by vigilant braves and squaws, petrified into natural sculpture? The figures would most likely be Mono Lake Paiutes, a tribe of Native Americans that lived here for centuries feeding off the lake's bounties. When

the Los Angeles authorities took over the surrounding streams to channel water into arid areas of Southern California, their age-old way of life was overthrown. Mono Lake became saturated with salt and its waters were left undrinkable.

Sara Wheeler

TIERRA DEL FUEGO

Tierra del Fuego is an archipelago that drips off the tail of South America. Separated from the Chilean and Argentinean mainland by the ice-choked waters of the Magellan Strait, the largest island is divided between the two republics by a vertical line drawn with a ruler. This is the bottom of the world, a sepulchral region where the curve on the globe turns steeply inwards.

Before I turned 30, some years ago, I found myself marooned at Puerto Williams on Isla Navarino, the southernmost permanent settlement in the world. I was at the end of a six-month journey through Chile. It had been a great time, my heart was fresh, and I had to get to Tierra del Fuego, the place where the whole world stopped. What could be more beguiling?

The land was first sighted by the navigator Ferdinand Magellan in 1520. Standing on the deck of his creaky wooden ship, he named what he saw Smokeland, after the wispy spires rising from the natives' fires. When he got home his patron, Charles V of Spain, announced that he preferred to call the place Fireland, presumably because there was no smoke without fire. And so it is. Nobody knew that Fireland was an archipelago. Francis Drake discovered that when he pushed past the icebergs in his own little ship 50 years later.

Navarino is Chilean now, and Williams its only village. The settlement was named after John Williams, the Bristolian captain of the Ancud, the ship that claimed the Magellan Strait for Chile in 1843. I too am from Bristol, so of course I felt at home. But Williams was a place where nothing ever happened. The low houses with their corrugated iron roofs were separated by dirt tracks carved with puddles. It's a harsh and frigid place: squeezed between three oceans, the Atlantic blows from the east, the Pacific from the west and the Southern Ocean from below. The westerlies in particular come freighted with mighty quantities of rain and snow. Even in summer, the temperature averages just 11°C and it's windy all the time.

One day, to pass the time, I went in an antediluvian lorry to deliver wood to a police station at the western tip of the island. We clunked across miles of deciduous southern beech forest, the silvery trunks swaddled in pale primrose lichen and twisted into alphabet configurations by the prevailing southwesterlies. A band of white mineral deposits circled every muddy pool, and their metallic whiff percolated the unheated cab.

The station consisted of a hut in a clearing that sloped down to the water's edge. It was an odd place for a police station, but Navarino lies directly below Argentinean territory, separated from it by a 12-mile strait. As the two countries existed in a permanently tensile state, the Chileans kept a keen eye out lest a marauding naval force were to surge over to claim the bounty of Navarino for Argentina. The station was served by three unarmed, untrained men, and it was difficult to imagine what they would do under these circumstances. But nobody worried too much about the detail down there.

At the end of the afternoon, as I was about to leave, the head policeman asked me if I'd care to stay for a while. My diary for that day notes, "Magritte clouds, beaver wigwams in the sphagnum bogs. No toothbrush. Must stay. What will I read?"

My carabineros took me mushroom picking, and taught me which ones were for eating. We fried them in butter with a bright orange spherical fungus we snapped off the beech trees. In the early morning, when the white cleaver-peaks of the Darwin Cordillera turned baby pink, we took the horses to patrol the desolate bays on the Beagle Channel to the south-west.

The horses stamped the tussock grass, steam dissolving off their coats into the chilly morning air, and lumpy steamer ducks careered over the rocks, redundant wings flapping irritably. We strolled about, and the policemen showed me where grass had grown over mounds of shells and ash left by the Yahgan Indians who used to paddle their beech-bark canoes from bay to bay, diving for shellfish and hunting seal. The name is westernized; they called themselves Yamana, which means "people". They were nomadic, and moved around the part of Tierra del Fuego that stretches from the Brecknock peninsula to Cape Horn, though their territory shrank as they were hunted by white men, and they ended up confined to the canals around Isla Navarino. They spoke five mutually intelligible dialects that together constituted a linguistic group unrelated to any other, and enjoyed one-word verbs meaning things like "to come unexpectedly across a hard substance while eating something soft" (like a pearl in an oyster). But they had no words for numerals beyond three: after you got to three, you just said "many".

The Yahgan were killed off by imported western diseases, and by European settlers who sliced off their ears in order to collect the reward offered for each dead Indian. The last pure Yahgan died in 1982.

When we rustled the gorse bushes, fat upland geese took off to the water, unfolding white-striped wings. To the south, the mountains trickled down into the ocean, lower and lower, the last visible remains of the longest range on earth – one that runs 4,300 miles from the Caribbean to Cape Horn, where it goes underwater. In the peaty light of early evening we rode towards the mountains called the Navarino Teeth in the heart of the island, a gleaming, uneven row of lower canines. Polar winds hurried across the ocean at that hour, and winter shouldered in from the south.

This was 15 years ago. When I think of it, costive at a desk behind the rain-splattered windows of home, staring into the sulphurous glow of London streetlights, I see the ghostly outlines of beech-bark canoes paddling eagerly from Wulaia to Douglas Bay. And I look back not just at a landscape I loved deeply. Shipwrecked now in another life, here where the curve on the globe is barely perceptible, I can just make out the hopes and dreams of a young woman I once knew, down there in Tierra del Fuego.

2. AIR

'As we hit the eyewall (of the hurricane), the winds climb rapidly, 90, 110, 125 knots, howling at the aeroplane from the left side. The plane starts to buck. Wind shears hammer the P-3 up and down; the rain is like a fire hose blasting the windows. The plane shakes so violently that the numbers on the instrument panel are unreadable. Yet, amidst the chaos, the voices on the intercom are calm and composed, people going about the business of science. One last updraft on the inner edge of the eyewall slams into the belly of the plane ... and suddenly all is calm. We're through the eyewall and into the eye, and the view is breathtaking. The surrounding wall of clouds, beautiful, menacing and awe-inspiring, looms tens of thousands of feet into the sky, encircling us, gently curving outward in a "stadium effect". Above us, clear blue sky; below, an angry sea whipped into a frenzy by howling winds.'

Commander Ron Philippsborn,
National Oceanic and Atmospheric Administration Corps P-3 'Hurricane Hunter' pilot

EARTH'S LARGEST OZONE HOLE

Recorded September 3, 2000
Location: Antarctic stratosphere
Fluctuating geographic coordinates

Earth's ozone depletion area (or ozone hole) was first measured only in 1985 but in recent years it has expanded to cover an area three times larger than the United States. On September 3, 2000, a NASA spectrometer detected the largest-ever Antarctic ozone depletion area, approximately 28.3 million square kilometres, up about 1 million square kilometres from two years earlier. For the moment at least, the swelling of the ozone hole (which peaks annually in the Southern Hemisphere's early spring) has nearly stabilized. But no one should take comfort in this shift.

Most atmospheric ozone is found in a band 19 to 30 kilometres above the earth's surface. This layer contains high concentrations of the bluish ozone gas, a gas that constitutes only about one-millionth of the atmosphere but that absorbs the sun's ultraviolet radiation more efficiently than any other substance. Without it, the increase in ultraviolet radiation that reaches Earth's surface would cause health disorders, damage plants and aquatic life, and drastically alter climates around the globe.

The great menace to the ozone layer is manufactured chemical gases (historically, chlorofluorocarbons, or CFCs), which interfere with ozone's molecular recombination when they hit ultraviolet rays. CFCs were banned worldwide in 1987 (in theory at least) by 24 countries, but the ozone hole continues to expand. Experts believe that even if we stop producing CFCs now, it will be decades before ozone holes are no longer an annual occurrence.

Ozone holes are seasonal, shrinking in summer and expanding over the poles in spring and winter. Our shrinking ozone layer has been tied to a higher incidence of skin cancer and cataracts, which can cause blindness. Many high-altitude animals, such as vicuñas, and people who live in arctic regions – southernmost Chile, for example – are also suffering.

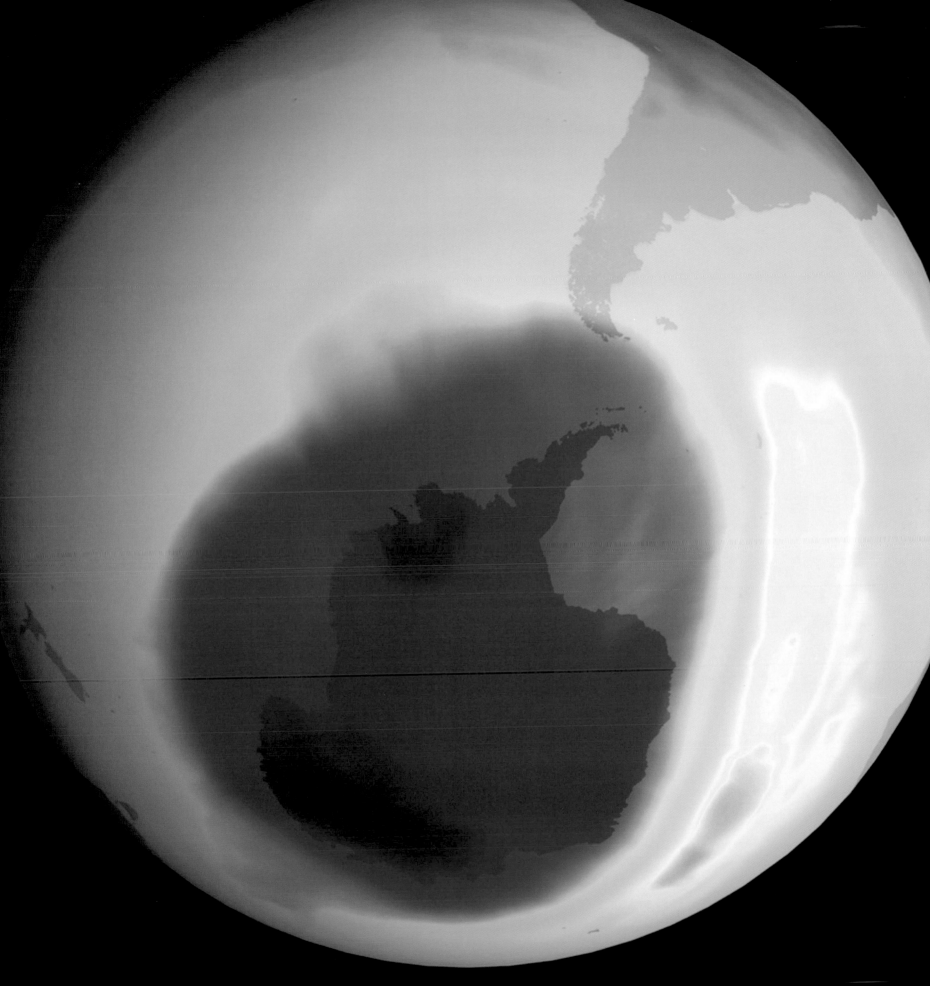

As with the global economy, so with Antarctica's ozone hole: problems originating in the North have more impact in the South. Two types of ozone depletion are at work, often attributed to human use of CFCs, also known as chlorofluorocarbons; the effect is to let in more ultraviolet radiation, harmful to life because it damages cellular DNA.

EARTH'S GREATEST LIGHT SHOWS

Aurora Borealis, Northern Hemisphere
Aurora Australis, Southern Hemisphere
Location: Polar regions
Fluctuating geographic coordinates

Named for the Roman goddess of dawn, auroras are electromagnetic halos to scientists, gigantic mood rings to poets.

To understand auroras, think of a television: an electron gun squirts electrons at a screen, which glows in various colours. In the upper atmosphere, 100 to 400 kilometres above ground, charged particles from the sun collide with atoms of oxygen and nitrogen, which glow in unearthly greenish-white and reddish colours and dance across the night skies.

There are three states of matter: solid, liquid, and gas. Water, for example, can exist as a *solid* block of ice, a puddle of *liquid*, and a *gas*, also known as steam. In these states, each atom has a central core surrounded by electrons. But 99 percent of the universe is not made of solid, liquid, or gas — it's made of plasma. Plasma is a very hot matter whose electrons have been ripped away from individual atoms, so that the cores of the atoms are left to float in a sea of electrons. Plasmas exist in flames, lightning bolts, plasma cutters in the local auto body shop, and, of course, the sun, which is like a giant hydrogen bomb throwing off about 1 million tonnes of charged particles each second. This is the "solar wind": a diluted plasma of charged electrons, hydrogen atom cores, and other really hot stuff.

Solar wind usually blows past Earth at about 400 kilometres per second. When Halley's Comet visited in 1986, its tail was always pointed directly away from the sun because it was blown that way by the power of the solar wind.

Earth is surrounded by a giant magnetic bubble shaped like a giant teardrop. On the side closest to the sun, this magnetic bubble is squashed by the solar wind, so it's quite close, about 60,000 kilometres away from the atmosphere. But on the side away from the sun, it's stretched by the solar wind, so that it reaches some 6 million kilometres downwind. This bubble protects Earth from high-speed charged particles from outer space, although it has holes at the North and South Magnetic Poles.

Auroras appear in three different situations. First, some of the solar wind gradually leaks into the magnetic bubble, which stretches and then suddenly snaps back, firing charged particles into the upper atmosphere near both poles, creating two simultaneous auroras.

Second, the corona, the sun's outer layer, squirts out giant bubbles of plasma, which become entangled with twisted magnetic fields. These enormous bubbles fly through space at 800 kilometres per second, and when they hit the upper atmosphere, they set off spectacular light shows.

Finally, the sun itself can squirt out an enormous blob of plasma registering about 1,000,000°C, at the amazing speed of 100,000 kilometres per second. Such a blob has enough energy to boil a lake hundreds of times the size of Australia. The sun squirts out these blobs several times each month, but luckily most of them miss us.

Dr Karl S. Kruszelnicki

The most common colour seen in auroras is a greenish white, from oxygen atoms, while nitrogen atoms give off a pink glow. Norwegian scientist Kristian Birkeland was first to explain the science of auroras, in the early 20th century, but these celestial phenomena are reflected in classical Greek and Chinese literature, the Old Testament and Norse sagas.

The Inuit call the lights *arsarnerit*, which translates as 'to play with a ball'. In ancient times, they believed that the auroras were their ancestors playing ball with a walrus skull and that the lights could be attracted to Earth

by whistling or repelled by barking like a dog. Auroras also hold spiritual significance to most northern peoples and are considered gifts from the dead to light up the long polar nights.

EARTH'S MOST ELECTRIFYING PLACE

Kampala, Uganda
Location: Central Africa
Coordinates: 00° 19′ 00″ N | 32° 35′ 00″ E

In classical mythology, thunderbolts were the emblem of the gods' power over Heaven and Earth. In Scandinavia, the blond-haired god Thor swinging his burning hammer caused lightning strikes; he travelled the skies in a chariot drawn by two male goats, and thunder was the sound of the wheels turning. The Nordic people loved Thor because when his chariot swept over the fields, the resulting rain gave them good crops. The Greeks believed that Zeus (Jupiter) ruled the sky and used lightning as his agent.

Just as this speedy, violent, sudden exchange of electrical energy has inspired myth, it has also sparked the scientific imagination. Lightning is a high-voltage electrical discharge between two charged rain clouds or between a cloud and the earth. It occurs when a thundercloud unleashes a negative electrical charge towards positive charges that have collected in other clouds and on the ground in buildings, boat masts, people,

flagpoles, mountaintops, and trees. A typical lightning flash lasts only a few tenths of a second. But in this flash of time, lightning superheats the surrounding air to a temperature five times hotter than on the surface of the sun. The nearby air expands and vibrates, forming thunder, but since sound travels more slowly than light, thunder is usually heard after lightning is seen. Each bolt of lightning heats the air around it to 30,000°C and can extend up to 30 kilometres. A typical lightning bolt is about 800 metres long.

There are about 70 to 100 lightning flashes per second worldwide, and 8 million bolts of lightning every day. Since lightning is linked to climate, with the highest occurrence in areas with frequent thunderstorms, the world's most electrifying area is also its most thundery: Kampala, Uganda, which has a thunderstorm 290 days a year on average.

'There are only three things that can kill a farmer: lightning, rolling over in a tractor, and old age.'

Bill Bryson

First came the accidental discovery by Luigi Galvani in 1786 that an electric shock could cause a dead frog's legs to twitch. Scientists today think that lightning actually 'switched on' evolution in the primal soup. By 2001, Pascal Simonet and his team, at the University of Lyons, France, used bolts of electricity to make bacteria swap DNA with one another.

Sir Ranulph Fiennes

POLAR

Antarctica is Earth's highest continent and also the driest; technically it's a desert. But because the air is very thin at the pole (10,000 metres), it feels like you're climbing at 4,900 metres in the Himalayas. It is so cold that when you blink, the fluid in your eyes can get caught on the lashes and freeze them together. You have to remove your hand from its glove so your fingers can melt and crush the ice balls on your eyelashes. After an expedition across Antarctica, you may have far fewer lashes than when you set out.

We started to cross the continent in November 1992. I weighed 98 kilogrammes pounds, and I was pulling a sled with food and supplies that weighed 219 kilogrammes. No one had ever completed an unsupported polar crossing carrying these extreme weights: it's the physical equivalent of running three marathons a day every day for 97 days without resting. As a result, you become very, very thin. We had been eating 5,000 calories per day, but our average output was 8,000 calories, so we were losing 3,000 calories daily. Whoever you're with needs to be tolerant because in a journey of this length, one or both of you are bound to get gangrene or crotch rot, both of which lead to extreme irritability.

My colleague, Dr. Mike Stroud, one of Europe's top physiologists, was studying stress nutrition. He would inject our bodies with some very expensive liquid, which subsequently, as urine, was placed into containers and whirled around in centrifuges, all of which was done in the tent.

Getting to the South Pole is a steady uphill incline of more than 3,000 metres across the continent. When I travel on an expedition like a polar traverse, I hope to see the opposite of what a tourist hopes for. A tourist would love beautiful scenery with

EARTH'S GREATEST SNOWFALLS

GREATEST DEPTH:
Tamarac, California, U.S.A., 1911
38° 26' 20" N | 120° 04' 30" W

GREATEST SINGLE SNOWSTORM:
Mount Shasta Ski Bowl, California, U.S.A., 1959
41° 19' 20" N | 122° 12' 07" W

A quick snow primer: Snow forms in the extremely cold upper reaches of clouds. A snowflake, or snow crystal, is a collection of supercooled water vapours and droplets that freeze around a microscopic nucleus. These snowflakes appear to be white because they act like prisms, scattering light in all directions, and they come in an infinite variety of shapes.

The greatest depth of snow accumulation ever recorded is 11.5 metres, which was measured in Tamarac, California, on March 11, 1911. The most snow produced in a single storm – a blizzard from February 13 to 19, 1959 – measured 4.8 metres at the Mount Shasta Ski Bowl in California.

'Nature has no mercy at all. Nature says, I'm going to snow.'

Maya Angelou

EARTH'S RAINIEST AND WETTEST PLACE

Mawsynram, Meghalaya
Location: North-east India
Coordinates: 25° 18′ 00″ N | 91° 35′ 00″ E

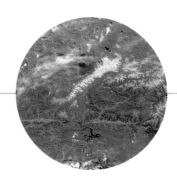

The average annual rainfall in Mawsynram, in the Meghalaya state of India (bordered on the north by the Himalaya range), measures about 12 metres. This amount of precipitation dwarfs that of places frequently considered to be "wet", such as Dublin, Ireland, which receives 73 centimetres; London, England, which receives 75 centimetres; New Orleans, Louisiana, 177 centimetres; Singapore, 215 centimetres; and Mount Waialeale, on the Hawaiian island of Kauai, which receives an average annual rainfall of about 10 metres and has 350 days of rain a year.

Not too long ago, the neighbouring area of Cherrapunji held the title of Earth's wettest spot, but climate changes have edged it out of its slot. Still it retains its natural beauty. Perched some 1,400 metres above sea level, Cherrapunji (right) looks down on the mist-shrouded valleys and churning rivers in the same Indian state of Meghalaya, the name of which translates as "the Abode of Clouds". Cherrapunji averages an annual rainfall of nearly 11 metres, drumming down hardest from May to September. In 1861 a record 23 metres of rain fell in one very soggy month.

These areas have just one season, the monsoon. Rain varies from heavy to medium to light, and it's one of the only places on Earth where rainfall is recorded in metres rather than centimetres. It most commonly rains at night.

EARTH'S WINDIEST PLACE

Commonwealth Bay
Location: South East Antarctica
Coordinates: 66° 54' 00" S | 142° 40' 00"

Antarctica is the world's highest, driest, coldest continent, but the most powerful feature of this brutal land is wind. Literally, wind is the lateral movement of the earth's atmosphere from high-pressure to low-pressure areas caused by the uneven heating of the sun. The most consistently windy place is Commonwealth Bay on the southern coast of East Antarctica. Here, katabatic winds (cold air pouring down glacial slopes) frequently exceed 306 kilometres per hour.

How powerful is a gust of this speed? Consider: Gale-force winds break branches and sweep you down the street. Hurricane winds begin at about 84 kilometres per hour and can reach upwards of 218 kilometres per hour. Katabatic winds have the force of a car wreck and, while not as speedy as those generated by some tornadoes, have extreme, earth-sculpting power.

By the time katabatic winds rage over Antarctica, they've been transformed from tropical, moisture-rich breezes to freezing, dry gusts that graze the central polar plateau and then race downhill, gaining speed before blasting the coast. They contribute to making the average annual temperature of Antarctica's elevated central plateau a frigid -55°C.

But even the gusts of Commonwealth Bay don't hold the record for the fastest surface wind. That blast tore through Mount Washington (altitude: 1,917 metres), New Hampshire, in the United States, at 372 kilometres per hour, on April 12, 1934. Earth's low-altitude wind-speed record – 333 kilometres per hour – was documented at the U.S. Air Force base at Thule, Greenland, on March 8, 1972.

'When the wind carries a cry which is meaningful to human ears, it is simpler to believe the wind shares with us some part of the emotion of Being than that the mysteries of a hurricane's rising murmur reduce to no more than the random collision of insensate molecules.'

Norman Mailer

This tent, torn down by the scything winds of Antarctica and half-buried in snow, illustrates the irresistible force of violent wind as it howls across the frozen continent. What little shelter it might have provided has gone – a reminder of

the extreme hardships endured by generations of polar explorers, and one that brings home the significance of Captain Oates's words as he left the Scott expedition's tent for the last time: 'I am just going outside and may be some time.'

EARTH'S COLDEST PLACE

Vostok Scientific Station
Location: Central East Antarctica
Coordinates: 78° 28' 00" S | 106° 49' 00" E

If Antarctica were a cocktail, it would be ice on the rocks. Ice covers about 98 percent of the land there. This constitutes 90 percent of the world's ice and 70 percent of the world's freshwater. The single largest piece of ice on Earth is the East Antarctic Ice Sheet, which is nearly 5 kilometres thick in some places. This is as thick as the European Alps are high. Earth's thickest ice (4,776 metres) was identified by echo-sounding aircraft in southern East Antarctica, not far from where in 1840 Lieutenant Charles Wilkes reported land and confirmed that Antarctica was a continent.

Antarctica's blue icebergs and sweeping glaciers make it a picturesque place. But the scenic Antarctic areas that tourists visit seasonally are mild compared with its elevated central plateau, where annual winter temperatures average between -50°C and -60°C. It is here, in a place called Plateau Station, that Earth's lowest sustained temperatures have been recorded. Note that the average annual temperature here is -57°C.

The world's lowest temperature was recorded in the Antarctic darkness during a storm on July 21, 1983. Within 150 kilometres of the South Geomagnetic Pole, Vostok Scientific Station registered -88°C. It's hard to imagine a chill this severe, yet it would seem toasty compared with the coldest temperature possible, absolute zero (-273°C), which is experienced only in deepest outer space.

Although it brings to mind a desolate expanse of flat, frozen sea, Vostok stands at an altitude of 3,500 metres and the air is thinner than it is at the Pole. Visitors find they can take only a few steps at a time; TV producer Jonathan Renouf recalls that this thin atmosphere made it impossible to record the Antarctic wind whistling round the base.

EARTH'S MOST INHOSPITABLE PLACE

Danakil Depression
Location: Eritrea/Ethiopia
Coordinates: 14° 00′ 00″ N | 40° 30′ 00″ E

The Danakil Depression is situated in an arid region of the Horn of Africa, known as Dankalia, where baking desert flatlands are broken up by isolated mountain groups and dry valleys spiked with thorny acacias. The lowland areas, once part of the Red Sea, are covered in vast salt plains interspersed with hot yellow sulphur fields.

No rain falls here for three-quarters of the year, and any meagre trickles escaping from higher ground are swallowed up in shallow saline lakes. A dry, scorching wind brings no relief from the heat and glare. The southern part of the region is of volcanic origin, a desolate zone of old lava flows and truncated cones. It is still prone to tremors, so that the earth itself shakes amid the shimmering

heat. The depression, reaching a depth of 120 metres below sea level, is also one of the hottest places on the planet because it is unusual to find such low-lying terrain not covered in water. As a result, air trapped in the depression can heat up to 50°C, as if in an oven.

Death Valley, in the U.S. state of California, runs Danakil a close second in terms of temperature. This parched area of dunes and volcanic rock, a major attraction for tourists, is capable of heating up 49°C. Here, too, you can find salt lakes, including the jagged terrain of the Devil's Golf Course, too rough for human players.

'What am I doing here?'

Rimbaud writing home from Ethopia

The nomadic Afar people have found ways to adapt to the murderous heat of the Danakil Depression. They live in hemispherical huts built from palm ribs and mats, sustaining life on a spartan diet of sour milk and dura flour porridge.

Patricia Moehlman

DANAKIL

Nur Heelo, a tall, slender man with sombre dignity and a resident of the Danakil Desert, once told me the following parable: A woman is standing with her young son on her hip in the midst of rising water. As the water rises she puts her son on her shoulder. The water rises again, and she places her son on her head. When the water rises yet again, she stands on her son. We had just been discussing the need for conserving wildlife, in particular the African wild ass in the Danakil, and his story was a gentle reminder that life here is very hard – so hard that if a person is to stay alive, terrible choices must often be made.

The Danakil Desert is the beginning of the Great Rift Valley in Africa, a dynamic geological fault that extends from the Red Sea far south to Zimbabwe. Standing on a high lava dike, looking east, the view is austere, arid, and frightening. It is a landscape with active volcanoes, long ridges of rough, sharp lava, and lower valleys covered in parched, alkaline soils.

In the Danakil water is crucial and rare (a year's rainfall varies from zero to 20 centimetres), and humans need to plan their work carefully. Even during the cooler months, from December through February, the temperature hovers at 46°C. For travellers from cooler, more temperate environments, it is a daunting terrain, but for the native Afar pastoralists it is home. Having worked as a biologist in this region for more than a decade, I have come to see the land as they do: with its blue jagged mountains and its valleys of pale sandy soil and slender grasses, it is stark but beautiful.

Historically, the Afar had a fierce reputation and caused fear among the people of the neighbouring highlands, as well as European explorers. But the terrain was ultimately more dangerous than the fearsome Afar, and many more travellers died from lack of water and food than from attack. Today, the Afar are shepherds who raise camels, sheep, and goats. Those who live near good water sources rear cattle. As nomads they lead their livestock to valleys that have had rain and where saline-tolerant grasses grow. Here, the rare *Acacia* trees are little more than shrubs, but they do provide forage and shade during the hottest time of the day.

Despite appearances to the contrary, the Danakil does have water for those who know how to find it. Near the Messir Plateau there is a spring-fed pond about 20 metres in diameter. The water is clean, and one can drink it without repercussions. The local Afar carefully remove the water from the pond then gently pour it into troughs for livestock, basins for laundry, and canvas bags for transport back to the village. Their temporary villages are comprised of dome-shaped huts with arched wood supports covered with woven mats. More permanent houses are rectangular frames covered with mats and grass thatching. Both buildings are cool and provide relief from the murderous sun. But for the men, women, and children who walk with the sheep and goats as they graze across the rocky slopes, the days are long. Projections for Africa are that in 25 years most of the continent will double in population. But in the Danakil, perhaps due to lack of resources and the harsh environment, the population is expected to remain static.

One of the animal world's most endangered species also calls the Danakil Desert home. The African wild ass (*Equus africanus*) ranges from the Red Sea in Eritrea to the Awash River in Ethiopia. It also lives in the Dallool Depression, one of the most desiccated places in the world. At more than 122 meters below sea level the substrate is very saline, and temperatures can hit 57°C. Here, one can find fossil sand dollars, a reminder that this land was once submerged below the waters of the Red Sea.

The African wild ass is a lean and muscular equid with a coat of short, slick grey hair that reflects the sun. It is the largest wild mammal in the desert, and its size, speed, and endurance inspire awe and respect among the local people. Unfortunately, they also mean that people attribute medicinal benefits to its organs, meat, and bones, which is one reason its population has been reduced 90% in the last two decades.

Still, conservation is making a difference. In Ethiopia, Afar leaders have banned the killing of any African wild ass. In Eritrea, the Afar have preserved the tradition of sharing their resources with wildlife, and the African wild ass is free to roam and feed and drink at the water sources. The life is hard and change occurs gradually, but as the local people say, *Kes ilu zikeyid bizuh yikeyid.* He who walks slowly, walks far.

EARTH'S MOST EXTREME SURFACE TEMPERATURES

Based on data from the National Climatic Data Centre's Global Measured
Extremes of Temperature and Precipitation. Place names verified through the
United States Board on Geographic Names and the National Imagery Mapping
Agency's (NIMA) geographic names database.

NOTE: 'Wet' precipitation figures for South America, Asia, and Antarctica
are for snow accumulation

NORTH AMERICA
HEAT: 134°F | DEATH VALLEY
ELEVATION: -178 ft | JULY 10, 1913
COLD: -81.4°F | SNAG, YUKON, CANADA
ELEVATION: 2120 ft | FEBUARY 3, 1947
WET: 256 in | AVERAGE OVER 14 YEARS
HENDERSON LAKE, BRITISH COLOMBIA | ELEVATION: 12 ft
DRY: 1.2 in | AVERAGE OVER 14 YEARS
BATAGUES, MEXICO | ELEVATION: 16 ft

SOUTH AMERICA
HEAT: 120°F | RIVADAVIA, ARGENTINA | ELEVATION: 676 ft | DECEMBER 11, 1905
COLD: -27°F | SARMIENTO, ARGENTINA | ELEVATION: 879 ft | JUNE 1, 1907
WET: 524 in | AVERAGE OVER 29 YEARS
LLORO, COLUMBIA | ELEVATION: 520 ft
DRY: <0.3 in | AVERAGE OVER 59 YEARS
ARICA, CHILE | ELEVATION: 95 ft

AFRICA
HEAT: 136°F | EL AZIZIA, LIBYA
ELEVATION: 367 ft | SEPTEMBER 13, 1922
COLD: -11°F | IFRANE, MOROCCO | ELEVATION:
5364 ft | FEBUARY 11, 1935
WET: 405 in | AVERAGE OVER 32 YEARS
DEBUNDSCHA, CAMEROON | ELEVATION: 30 ft
DRY: <0.1 in | AVERAGE OVER 39 YEARS
WADI HALFA, SUDAN | ELEVATION: 410 ft

EUROPE

HEAT: 122°F | SEVILLE, SPAIN | ELEVATION: 26 ft | AUGUST 4, 1881
COLD: -67°F | UST'SHCHUGOR, RUSSIA | ELEVATION: 279 ft | JANUARY
(EXACT DATE UNKNOWN, LOWEST IN 15-YEAR PERIOD)
WET: 183 in | AVERAGE OVER 25 YEARS
CRKVICA, BOSNIA-HERZEGOVINA | ELEVATION: 3,337 ft
DRY: 6.4 in | AVERAGE OVER 13 YEARS
ASTRAKHAN, RUSSIA | ELEVATION: 45 ft

AUSTRALIA

HEAT: 128°F | CLONCURRY, QUEENSLAND | ELEVATION: 622 ft | JANUARY 16, 1889
COLD: -9.4°F | CHARLOTTE PASS, NSW | ELEVATION: 5,758 ft | JUNE 29, 1994
WET: 340 in | AVERAGE OVER 9 YEARS
BELLENDEN KER, QUEENSLAND | ELEVATION: 5,102 ft |
DRY: 4.05 in | AVERAGE OVER 42 YEARS
MULKA (TROUDANINNA), SOUTH AUSTRALIA | ELEVATION: 160 ft |

ASIA

HEAT: 129°F | TIRAT TSVI, ISRAEL
ELEVATION: -722 ft | JUNE 21, 1942
COLD: -90°F | OIMYAKON, RUSSIA
ELEVATION:2,625 ft | FEBUARY 6, 1933
COLD: -90°F | VERKHOYANSK, RUSSIA
ELEVATION: 350 ft | FEBUARY 7, 1892
WET: 467.4 in | AVERAGE OVER 38 YEARS
MAWSYNRAM,INDIA | ELEVATION: 4,597 ft
DRY: 1.8 in | AVERAGE OVER 50 YEARS
ADEN, YEMEN | ELEVATION: 22 ft

ANTARCTICA

HEAT: 59°F | VANDA STATION
ELEVATION: 49 ft | JANUARY 5, 1974
COLD: -129°F | VOSTOK
ELEVATION: 11,220 ft | JULY 21, 1983
DRY: 0.8 in | AVERAGE OVER 10 YEARS
AMUNDSEN-SCOTT, SOUTH POLE STATION
ELEVATION: 9,186 ft |

EARTH'S MOST POWERFUL TORNADOES

FASTEST: Bridge Creek, Oklahoma, U.S.A., 1999
Coordinates: 35° 14' 06" N | 97° 44' 11" W

MOST DEADLY: Tri-State (U.S.A.) Tornado, 1925
From south-eastern Missouri, across southern Illinois, and into south-western Indiana

BIGGEST: Super Tornado Outbreak, 1974
Coordinates: Across 13 U.S. states

The roaring, swirling winds of a tornado sound like a freight train. That is, when they're not tearing through a town near you, in which case, you'd be running too fast to think about what this violent column of air sounds like. The average tornado is 200 metres wide and advances at about 50 kilometres per hour. Rarely do twisters travel farther than 10 kilometres. But even these brief weather phenomena have more destructive power than other kinds of storms. India, Australia, Russia, and Argentina are among the nations that experience tornadoes, but the United States has the most and the strongest twisters on Earth: an average of 800 a year, resulting in 80 deaths and more than 1,500 injuries.

Twisters (as well as hail and strong winds) develop when cold, dry air and warm, moist air collide to produce a thunderstorm. About 1 percent of all thunderstorms in the United States spawn a tornado. When strong winds blow over weak ones, creating an invisible, horizontal spinning effect in the lower atmosphere, a wind shear develops beneath this storm. A strong updraft can catch the wind shear, lifting and twisting it at the same time. If upper-level winds propel this cyclone forward so that it touches the ground, a tornado is born. Wherever they land, they can suck up and spit out cars, buses, houses, livestock, and forests.

The highest wind speeds ever recorded in a tornado were measured on May 3, 1999, in a tornado that passed near Bridge Creek, Oklahoma, in the United States, twisting at 508 kilometres per hour. The world's most violent or deadly twister was the Tri-State Tornado, which ripped across the U.S. states of Missouri, Illinois, and Indiana in 1925. Over three and a half hours, its ground speed averaged 100 kilometres per hour along a 350-kilometre path of destruction, the longest ground track of any tornado. It killed 695 people and injured 2,027 others, causing millions of dollars in damages.

As deadly as this tornado was, it was minor compared with the Super Tornado Outbreak on April 3-4, 1974, in which 148 twisters spun across 13 U.S. states. After 16 hours, 315 people were dead and 5,300 were injured in a path of damage more than 4,000 kilometres long. During the peak, 15 tornadoes were on the ground at the same time, six of which had winds reaching 420 to 514 kilometres per hour.

In *Heaven's Breath – A Natural History of the Wind*, author Lyall Watson notes that tornadoes have left records 'of horses being carried 3 kilometres and set down unharmed, and of others left considerably surprised astride a barn ... Milkmaids have been left with nothing but the bucket as the wind carried their cow away; and on one memorable

occasion a whole herd of cattle were seen drifting off together, 'looking like giant birds in the sky'. But their savagery is savage indeed: 'Human beings and animals are often beheaded, impaled by flying timber, maimed and mutilated, stripped of their clothing, and spewed out of the funnel, their naked bodies made hideous by a jet-black incrustation of mud.'

EARTH'S GREATEST TREE LOSS BY WINDSTORM

December 26-27, 1999
Location: Across France
A range of geographic coordinates: Paris 48° 50′ N | 02° 20′ E

Just a day after Christmas, on December 26, 1999, parts of France were nearly flattened by the Lothar windstorm that devastated millions of acres of forest, threatened its timber industry, and left thousands without electricity for weeks. In the early-morning hours, a large weather system rotating around a low-pressure centre, much like a hurricane, blew across western Europe with winds as high as 219 kilometres per hour. The storms hit the coast of France at the tip of Brittany, passed by Le Havre and Rouen, and arrived in the Paris area with gusts clocked at 173 kilometres per hour. They ripped slabs of roofing from Notre Dame cathedral and blew stonework through a stained-glass window at Sainte-Chapelle. Outside Paris, the palace of Versailles took a beating: windows were smashed, and some 6,000 trees in the palace's gardens were uprooted. The storm system later blew across Germany and Austria, but France suffered the most severe blows. The winds flattened 1.2 million acres – 360 million trees – and more than 741,000 others were severely damaged. Within 30 hours, the storm caused 87 deaths and a fortune in damages.

Another tremendous tree loss was documented around the remote Russian area of Tunguska, Siberia, in 1908. Although the cause of the destruction was probably a large meteorite that exploded as it hit the upper atmosphere, a torrential blast filled the skies and flattened trees across an area twice the size of Luxembourg. The explosion was heard 1,000 kilometres away, but no one was killed. But because no one bothered to count all the fallen trees, the French event holds the record.

EARTH'S MOST DESTRUCTIVE HURRICANES

BIGGEST: Hurricane Mitch (November 24-27, 1998)
Location: Central America (area of greatest rainfall: La Ceiba, Honduras)
Coordinates: 15° 44′ N | 86° 52′ W

MOST EXPENSIVE: Hurricane Andrew (1992)
Location: Bahamas, Florida, and Louisiana

A gentle breeze that rustles leaves and sets tree branches swaying measures 21 to 29 kilometres per hour. Stronger winds measuring 39 to 49 kilometres per hour may whistle through telephone wires, whip up white caps, and set whole trees in motion.

A hurricane – the name comes from the Carib Indian word *urican*, which means "big wind" – describes a storm with winds upwards of 119 kilometres per hour. In an average year, six tropical storms build to hurricane strength in the Atlantic Ocean. The terrible power of sustained winds of this speed – strong enough to carry away people, cars, and buildings – is compounded by waves of water. The average hurricane drops more than 9 trillion litres of rain each day, causing massive floods and coastal washouts. Ninety percent of all hurricane-related deaths are caused by storm surges – waves that can rise 7.5 metres above the ocean's surface.

The biggest hurricane in modern times was Hurricane Mitch, which hit Central America in 1998 and caused over 11,000 deaths, destroyed 93,690 dwellings, and left about 2.5 million people dependent on international aid. Wind speeds reached 290 kilometres per hour as the storm blasted westward from Jamaica and the Cayman Islands to Honduras, Nicaragua, El Salvador, Guatemala, Costa Rica, and then north to Mexico's Yucatán Peninsula, east to Florida, and finally to the Bahamas. In Honduras alone, 6,500 people died, and damages exceeded US$5 billion. The only Western Hemisphere hurricane to surpass Mitch in ferocity was the Great Hurricane of October 10-16, 1780, which killed approximately 22,000 people in the eastern Caribbean.

The most damaging hurricane ever occurred on August 24, 1992, when Hurricane Andrew battered the Bahamas, Florida, and Louisiana, racking up a toll of about US$26.5 billion. Andrew's winds whipped at 233 kilometres per hour during landfall over Florida, caused 26 deaths, and left 250,000 people temporarily without homes. The 1926 Great Miami Hurricane was even more devastating. With adjustments for inflation, growth, and wealth changes, this hurricane would have caused destruction estimated at US$70 billion in Florida plus another US$10 billion of damage in neighbouring regions.

An average hurricane drops some 20 billion tonnes of water a day, the energy equivalent of a half million atom bombs. And while their wind speeds may fall short of tornadoes, they are a thousand times more powerful. This scene shows the aftermath of Cyclone George, which ravaged Santo Domingo, capital of the Dominican Republic, on September 28, 1998.

EARTH'S WORST TROPICAL CYCLONES

LONGEST-LASTING: Hurricane/Typhoon John (August and September 1994)
Location: Pacific Ocean

DEADLIEST: Bangladesh Cyclone (November 1970)
Coordinates: 24° 00′ 00″ N | 90° 00′ 00″ E

In the Atlantic Ocean, low-pressure tropical storms are called *hurricanes*. When they form over the Bay of Bengal and in the Indian Ocean or around Australia, they're called *cyclones*. When they form in the western Pacific Ocean, they're known as *typhoons*. Regardless of what they're called, these storm systems occur mainly near the equator, in regions with prevailing easterly winds, and they can bring life-threatening winds and water. Although tornadoes are more intense than hurricanes or cyclones, they tend to be less destructive because of their short life spans. A hurricane or cyclone can roil over the oceans for weeks and, when it hits land, can send a wave of destruction over thousands of kilometres.

The most deadly tropical cyclone occurred in Bangladesh in November 1970. Winds coupled with a storm surge killed at least 300,000 people, primarily as a result of the storm's tide surge over low-lying deltas. Another deadly cyclone struck the delta regions of Bangladesh in 1991, killing more than 138,000 people and causing damage in excess of US $1.5 billion. The tropical cyclone devastated the coastal area south-east of Dacca with gale winds and a 6-metre storm surge.

Scientists fear that windstorms and hurricanes could become more frequent and intense from global warming. Rising temperatures could lead to changes in regional wind systems that would wreak havoc with global rainfall and lead to the redistribution and frequency of floods, droughts, and forest fires. It's entirely possible that a warmer world will be a windier world, and even more extreme hurricanes could be on the way.

The longest-lasting tropical cyclone in the Eastern Hemisphere was named Hurricane John; it lasted for 31 days as it coursed through both the north-east and north-west Pacific basins during August and September 1994. Curiously, the storm was renamed Typhoon John as soon as it crossed the international date line; after changing course and recrossing the date line, its name reverted to Hurricane John. Because John's title changed twice, some consider Hurricane Ginger (1971) in the North Atlantic to be officially the world's longest-lasting cyclone, but John lasted three days longer.

Sebastian Junger

STORM

The most overwhelming force of nature I've witnessed was the storm that hit the north shore of Massachusetts. I was living in Gloucester at the time, and I saw 40-foot-high waves rolling in, detonating against the mansions on the shore. Those waves looked like they were moving so slowly, yet they were unstoppable. It was thrilling and terrifying, and it resulted in a book. It also made me absolutely aware of the fact that nature really is in control. It just doesn't care.

A lot of Western societies, America in particular, have a tremendous arrogance about what they think they control, nature included. Although there aren't many natural catastrophes in the United States, when they do occur – say a landslide – there is this misplaced indignation with which we ask: How could this happen to us?

There are few places in the world where people become so indignant. Perhaps they're sorrowful, but they don't feel entitled to any special dispensation in the animal kingdom. We Americans do imagine that, and it says a lot about us.

We should be thankful that America has never suffered an earthquake like the one in Turkey that killed 20,000 people or a Colombian-size mudslide that buried over 20,000. The worst natural disaster of the last century was the Galveston, Texas, flood of 1900, which wiped out roughly 6,000 people.

In fact, when a natural event of overwhelming force occurs, for a brief while it reminds us of our relative insignificance. Only people who imagine themselves to be giants striding the earth can understand the importance of occasionally being shown to be so small.

.FIR

3

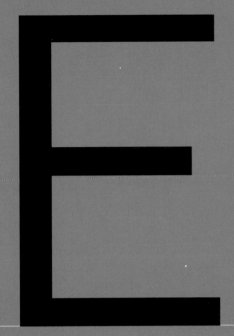

'We saw a green sun, and such a green as we have never,
either before or since, seen in the heavens. We saw smears and
patches of something like verdigris green in the sky, and they
changed to equally extreme blood red, or to coarse brick-dust
reds, and in an instant passed to the colour of tarnished
copper of shining brass ... Nearly the entire western half of
the horizon has changed to a fiery crimson: as time goes on,
the northern and southern areas lose their glory, and the greys
of night contract, from the northern end, most rapidly; the
east is of normal grey. The south now closes in, and a glow
comes up from the west like that of white-hot steel, reddening
somewhat as it mounts to the zenith.'

Report of the Krakatoa committee of the Royal Society, 1888

Haraldur Sigurdsson

At the dawn of man, volcanoes were regarded as manifestations of evil forces hidden deep in the earth. Gods, giants or spirits were held responsible for eruptions and earthquakes, especially in the world's most volcanically active regions such as Polynesia, Indonesia, Iceland, and Italy.

Among the Polynesian people of the Tonga islands, for instance, the great hero Maui lurked deep in the netherworld and was the keeper of fire. Maui slept in a cave and, if he turned over in his dreams, an earthquake shook the land above.

Should Vesuvius blow in southern Italy, locals still call on Saint Gennaro, who acquired his protective aura when he was thrown to the lions at nearby Pozzuoli and the lions refused to eat him – a temporary reprieve, as the Romans later beheaded him. Thereafter he became patron saint of Naples.

To this day, whenever Vesuvius erupts, his remains are paraded to the foot of the volcano to placate the evil powers within. Twice a year, his blood, stored in a vial at Naples' cathedral, is said to liquefy and bubble. In May and December, believers ceremoniously invert the vial: a good omen if the blood within moves along the glass; if not, an augury of eruption.

The ancient Greeks were the first to explain eruptions as an escape of winds from within the earth. Hesiod's poem *Theogony* describes the battle between Zeus and the Titans in terms strikingly similar to an earlier description of the eruption on the island of Thira (Santorini), one of the largest eruptions in the Mediterranean ever.

The Romans first hatched the idea that combustion was taking place within the earth, causing other materials to melt and so unleash an eruption. That theory held sway right through until the 17th and 18th centuries, when scientists reached the more accurate view that earth's interior is very hot and volcanic activity releases molten material through vents in the surface.

Today it's both thrilling and terrifying to realize that we don't really know, nor can we predict, when the next big eruption will occur. All we do know is that a "supereruption" will occur every 50,000 to 100,000 years. Techniques such as radar interferometry — a satellite radar system — can scan the earth's surface but cannot yet read volcanoes.

Another problem is that geologists tend to monitor only those volcanoes that have erupted in the past — not much help for prediction, as the next supervolcano is unlikely to have erupted before. Indeed, the next to erupt may have lain dormant for a thousand years or not even be recognized as a volcano, as happened in 1951 in Papua New Guinea. Here no one even recognized Mount Lamington as a volcano until it erupted and killed many.

One of the best ways to compare past eruptions is to measure the amount of material ejected. Mount St. Helens made headlines worldwide by hurling out 1 or 2 cubic kilometres, but the eruption was relatively small in historical terms. Vesuvius in 79 C.E. was five times as big, spewing out some 5 cubic kilometres. Krakatoa produced twice as much again, and the roar of its explosion was so loud that if it had happened in Boston, it would have been heard both in London and Los Angeles.

For an eruption of a different order of magnitude, we must go back to Tambora in 1815. This massive convulsion, the largest in recorded history, ejected 100 cubic

Ash and other gases created a pall that bounced back the sun's rays, bringing global cooling and severe crop failure for at least three years.

kilometres, or 10 times the amount of Krakatoa. It is a big volcano, steep and difficult to access, but it's been exciting to unravel its story and fascinating to study its workings in depth as we dig in further.

The eruption was so large that it killed 117,000 people. A tribe living on mountain slopes in North Tambora up the coast was exterminated and its language lost forever. Our studies have shown that this cataclysmic event belched about 100 times more chlorine into earth's atmosphere than the current output of the same gas from human activity, now a cause of much concern because of the destruction of the ozone layer. Ash and other gases from Tambora created a pall that bounced back the sun's rays, bringing global cooling and severe crop failure for at least three years.

The three largest eruptions in North America of the past few million years occurred in Yellowstone. They poured out so much magma that the earth's crust collapsed into the magma chamber under the weight, forming calderas. Yellowstone and Toba ejected some 2,000 cubic kilometres of material, 20 times as much as Tambora.

We have only an inkling of how such an event might affect today's technology-dependent society but we do know it would cause significant global cooling. Ash floating in the jet stream and the stratosphere would make aviation impossible, and telecommunications would collapse because of interference with satellite and microwave transmissions. Pyroclastic flows and surges extending for thousands of kilometres would obliterate agriculture and politically destabilize the region.

EARTH'S LARGEST FLOOD BASALTS

Siberian Traps, Russia (2 million km²)
Coordinates: 64° 10' 00" N | 99° 55' 00" E

Deccan Traps, India (500,000 km²)
Coordinates: 14° 00' 00" N | 77° 00' 00" E

Laki Basalt, Iceland (565 km²)
Coordinates: 64° 04' 00" N | 18° 14' 00" W

When magma is released from Earth's mantle, it is very hot and runny, composed of rocks that melt easily. When it solidifies, it forms basalt rock.

The most dramatic basaltic lava flows don't come from volcanic cones but emerge from fissures that can run for several kilometres. The world's largest flood basalt, the Siberian Traps, formed about 250 million years ago and covers an area bigger than Europe. The volume of the Siberian Traps, near the city of Tura in northern Russia, is probably large enough to cover the entire surface of the earth to a depth of 3 metres. Because the traps were created at the same time as the largest mass extinction (at the end of the Permian period, when up to 95 percent of the existing species disappeared), scientists believe that the climate-altering emission of ash and gases of the Siberian Traps could have played a lethal role. Other immense and ancient flood basalts include the Deccan Traps (right) in west-central India (most of which erupted between 65 million and 60 million years ago), which in some areas are as much as 2,000 metres deep.

The two largest flood-basalt-producing eruptions in recorded history were in Iceland. The first occurred after the eruption of Eldgja in 935 C.E.; then in 1783 the Laki fissure spewed out 15 cubic kilometres in a eruption that lasted for six months and caused noticeable atmospheric cooling. The volcanic haze killed crops (through the acid rain it created) and livestock (by poisoning), eventually starving to death 9,000 people, or one-fifth of Iceland's population at that time.

Almost inconceivably vast compared with ordinary volcanic events, flood basalt eruptions are rare – only eight have occurred in the last 250 million years. They are triggered by a 'mantle plume', a giant pulse of heat rising from the boundary of the earth's core that helps to cool the molten core. The Deccan Traps (above) are in west-central India.

Mount Ararat is singled out in the Bible as the landing place for Noah's Ark at the close of the Great Flood: a patch of divinely ordained dry land after 40 days and nights of deluge. Geologically, Mount Ararat is a harsher place: this

imposing basalt boulder, so reminiscent of curved ship timbers, was blasted from the ancient volcano in the Aras Mountains of eastern Turkey – more a sign of the primordial rages of Mother Earth perhaps than of God the Father

EARTH'S MOST ACTIVE VOLCANO

Stromboli
Location: Lipari Islands, Tyrrhenian Sea, Italy
Coordinates: 38° 47' 00" N | 15° 13' 00" E

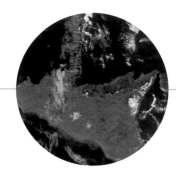

While Hawaii's Kilauea gets a lot of attention for its constant flow of lava, it is only a drop in the volcanic bucket compared with that of Stromboli, off the coast of southern Italy, which has been heaving continuously for more than 2,000 years. Stromboli, which looms 927 metres over the Lipari Islands in the Tyrrhenian Sea and has several craters, is the earth's most hotheaded volcano.

Emitting hot sulphurous vapours and small gas explosions hourly, ejecting glowing cinder and lava bombs hundreds of metres into the air, and occasionally producing small streams of lava, Stromboli is an object of mythical pride. In ancient times, local islanders revered the volcano as a fire god and regarded their land as the mythical residence of Aeolus, the wind god. Stromboli is also called "the lighthouse of the Mediterranean".

Despite its apparent fury, Stromboli's eruptions are rarely violent. Nonetheless, in 1919, four people were killed and 12 homes destroyed by huge blocks of hot rock, some of which weighed 50 tonnes. In 1930, three people were killed by pyroclastic flows, and another person was boiled to death in the sea near the point where the lava flowed into the ocean. Those explosions gave off as much ash as that produced during five years of normal activity.

Strabo, a Greek geographer, described nearby Vulcano as 'the island of fire with three breaths emerging from three

craters'. Stromboli, active for over two millennia (shown above), had 'less violent flames' but 'more resounding rumbles'.

EARTH'S OLDEST ACTIVE VOLCANO

Mount Etna
Location: Sicily, Italy
Coordinates: 37° 45′ 00″ N | 15° 00′ 00″ E

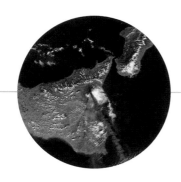

Long ago, some god must have done something very naughty to send Mount Etna into a perpetual fury. The rage of this volcano has inspired and infuriated poets, artists and historians since antiquity.

At about 3,353 metres high, Mount Etna (right), in Sicily, is Europe's tallest active volcano. Its name comes from the Greek *aitho*, for "I burn", and its first eruption was recorded in 1500 B.C.E. Since then, it has blown at least 190 times. The ancient poet Hesiod wrote about Etna's eruptions. Plato sailed from Greece in 387 B.C.E. just to gaze at it. Odysseus was said to dodge boulders flung by a cyclops on top of it. The Romans considered it Vulcan's forge and the resting place of the giant Enceladus (eruptions were marks of his breath, and earthquakes signalled his movements). Of the later eruptions, those in 1169 and 1669 were the most

destructive, but it was the earthquakes, not the rivers of burning lava, that caused the most damage. Because the outbursts occurred at the upper part of the mountain where lava moves slowly, Etna is not a killer volcano, and it rarely takes human lives. This is why it is known as the "friendly giant".

Etna has three ecological zones. The base supports a rich variety of subtropical vegetation, including citrus, bananas, olives, and figs. At more temperate altitudes, vineyards and various stone-fruit trees flourish. Higher still are chestnut, birch, and pine woods, and above this is a desolate waste of lava and ash. Near the top, snow collects for most of the year. Always smoking, Etna – which covers 1,600 square kilometres and has a circumference of about 150 kilometres – has been increasingly active in the past 50 years.

Etna's June 2001 eruption vomited up an ash plume that reached the Sahara. Lava fountains shot 400 m into the air and hurled lava bombs the size of cars. Scientists described the sound of bubbling lava as a 'strident clicking, like glass rubbing glass' and noticed 'a dark rumbling below ground' that they felt 'in their teeth'.

EARTH'S LARGEST ACTIVE VOLCANO AND FASTEST-RECORDED LAVA FLOW

Mauna Loa
Location: Island of Hawaii ("Big Island"), Hawaii, U.S.A.
Coordinates: 19° 28' 56" N | 155° 36' 18" W

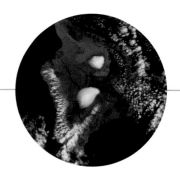

Mauna Loa is the world's largest mountain, with a mass of 80,000 cubic kilometres. It also is the world's largest active volcano. Since its period of greatest activity in 1881, it has erupted four times, in 1942, 1949, 1975, and 1984. Its crater and caldera are the world's second largest, with an area of 9.6 square kilometres.

Only 4,169 metres of the mountain are above sea level, but Mauna Loa is an extremely wide-based shield volcano, a typical Hawaiian variety that forms when hot lava oozes from fissures in the earth's crust. Shield volcanoes differ from explosive, cone-shaped peaks like Mount Etna, in that they are sprawling, low-angled

mountains built from basalt. Seamounts, or islands that form from shield volcanoes, originate far beneath the ocean's surface and steadily build over millions of years. Hawaii's Big Island is composed of five distinct volcanoes that blended together to form a single island.

In 1950 Mauna Loa also spewed out the fastest lava flow ever recorded: 9.3 kilometres per hour. But conventional measurements of speed didn't exist at the time of some of the earth's greatest eruptions, such as the 12-hour blast at Vesuvius in 79 B.C.E., which entombed local inhabitants in a huge shell of pyroclastic ash as they were running for their lives.

'We walk on molten lava on which the claw of a fly or the fall of a hair makes its impression, which being received, the mass hardens to flint and retains every impression forevermore.'

Ralph Waldo Emerson

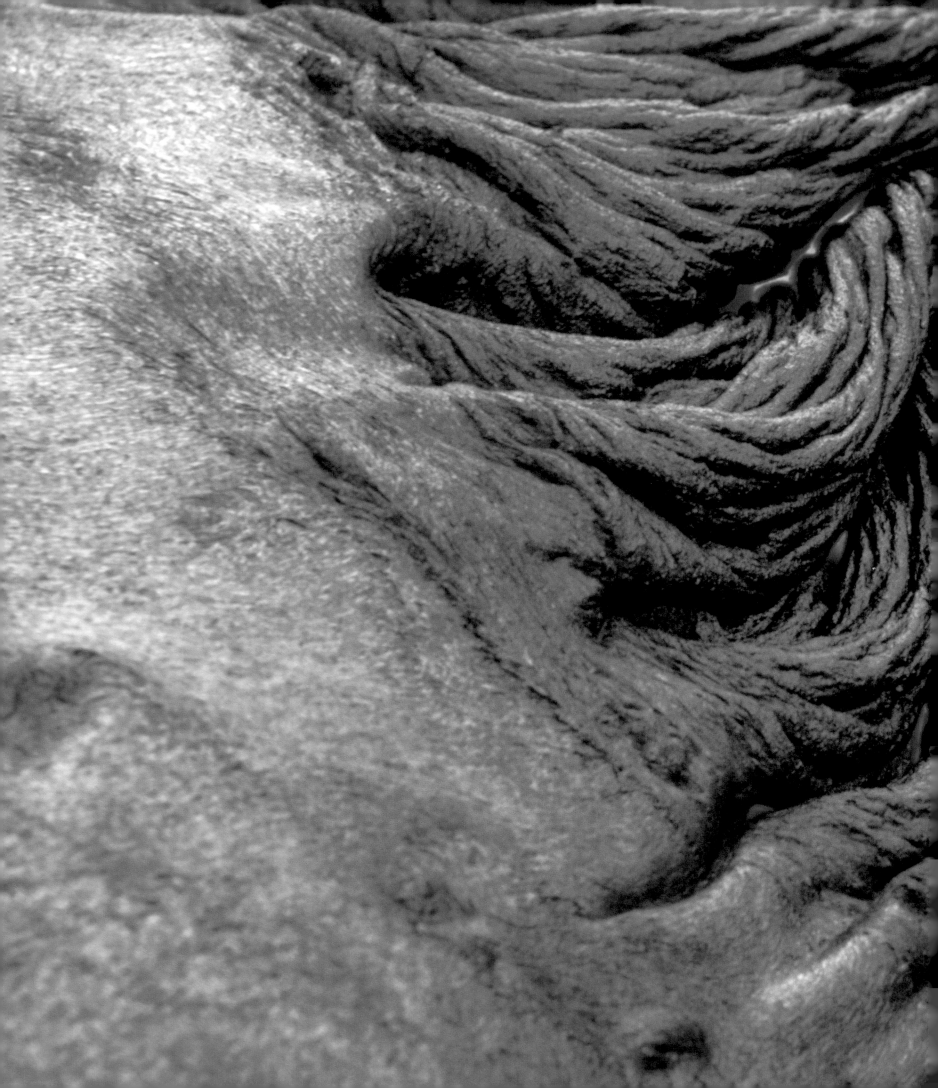

EARTH'S YOUNGEST AND FASTEST-GROWING VOLCANO

Parícutin
Location: Central Mexico
Coordinates: 19° 28' 00" N | 102° 15' 00" W

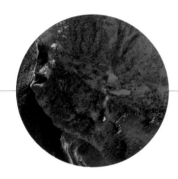

The birth of a volcano can be terrible or beautiful, depending on how it is perceived – and from what distance.

On the afternoon of February 20, 1943, in the Mexican state of Michoacán, the Parícutin volcano was born in a fury of thunder, ash, sulphur fumes, and smoke. Across nearly featureless farmland that began the day as a flat field, a huge fissure appeared. It ripped open a vent in the earth that gave birth to a rock-hurling edifice that grew 46 metres tall in only 24 hours. The instant appearance of a 15-story-tall mountain was a sight beyond belief, but the worst was yet to come. On the second night, the volcano hurled glowing bombs more than 305 metres into the black sky,

and fiery fingers of lava began to run through the surrounding cornfields. Over the next nine years, Parícutin grew with few interruptions, spewing out more than a billion tonnes of lava, until February 1952, when the volcano simply stopped as suddenly as it began.

Parícutin gave the modern world its first opportunity to witness the birth of such a lava spewer. In its first year, its cone topped 336 metres – or about the height of the Eiffel Tower – and ash destroyed and suffocated almost all the vegetation for several metres around the crater. Pyroclastic ash buried the town of San Juan Parangaricutiro and the village of Parícutin.

Parícutin intruded on a peaceful field, taking the locals and the scientific world by surprise, but two signs foretold its birth. About 300 earthquakes shook the ground the day before the volcano began its rise. And local lore recounts a locust plague of biblical proportions in 1942

EARTH'S LARGEST ACTIVE CRATER

Halemaumau Crater, on Kilauea
Location: Island of Hawaii ("Big Island"), Hawaii, U.S.A.
Total Size: 76 m wide, 122 m long, and a floor covering 38 ha
Coordinates: 19° 24′ 00″ N | 155° 17′ 00″ W

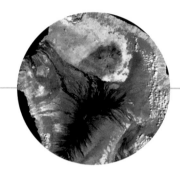

According to legend, the fire goddess Pele lives at the bottom of the Halemaumau crater, and her mood is signalled by the amount of lava that pours out. Others refer to the crater as the "House of Everlasting Fire", because between 1823 and 1924, this was basically a bubbling cauldron of molten lava.

Halemaumau crater is both vast and fiery. Seen from above, it no longer looks like a steaming pot of chunky red curry. Time has cooled it so that it's more like a Martian landscape, a brown, rocky, surprisingly wide plain that encloses a steaming depression, charred black in the middle, like a burned-out barbecue pit. Visitors can get extremely close to the crater, by foot and by car.

Kilauea is one of the world's most active volcanoes. Over 90 percent of its surface is covered by lava less than 1,000 years old, which almost continuously poured out between 1823 and 1924. Since then, only one interval of more than four years has separated its eruptions, and the current flow, spewing from Kilauea's Pu'u O'o vent, has been seeping towards the town of Kalapana since 1983. It shows no sign of easing up.

The Pu'u O'o flow (right) started as shooting jets of glowing lava but has now settled into a constant river of lava that would cover a 9-metre-deep, four-lane highway stretching the entire length of the U.S.A. Molasses-like globs of lava ooze out at temperatures of 260°C before cooling into a crust at the surface.

EARTH'S LARGEST VOLCANIC ERUPTIONS

Yellowstone Caldera: North America (2 million years ago)
Vesuvius, Italy (79 C.E.): 40° 49' 00" N | 14° 26' 00" E
Tambora, Indonesia (1815): 08° 14' 00" S | 117° 55' 00" E
Krakatoa, Indonesia (1883): 06° 07' 00" S | 105° 24' 00" E
Mount Pelée, Martinique, West Indies (1902): 14° 48' 00" N | 61° 10' 00" W
Novarupta, Alaska, U.S.A. (1912): 58° 15' 55" N | 155° 09' 29" W

No one knows which of Earth's countless volcanic eruptions was the largest. When the Yellowstone Caldera erupted 2 million years ago, it supposedly ejected 1 million cubic metres of ash, cinders, blocks, and lava in a plume that shot 25 kilometres into the air – the equivalent height of three Mount Everests stacked on top of one another. This is still thought to be the world's most powerful explosion, but these measurements are only estimates.

One of history's most powerful and deadly eruptions famously occurred at Vesuvius (right), near Naples, Italy, at 8.32am on August 24, 79 C.E., burying Pompeii, Herculaneum, and Stabiae under cinders, ashes, and mud. This massive two-minute blast shook the earth, shot out rock, volcanic glass, and steam, and triggered an avalanche that demolished the cone. A plume of pyroclastic ash rose as high as the Yellowstone Caldera's eruption, and lightning generated by this superheated ash cloud sparked forest fires. During the day, nearly 540 million tons of ash fell over 57,000 square kilometres. At least 16,000 people died, including Pliny the Elder, a Roman naturalist who had come to investigate the eruption.

To give you an idea of the destructive force of these so-called Plinian eruptions, Vesuvius, which had been 1,277 metres high, lost 400 metres in height in one day. Because of the frequent eruptions of varying severity on Vesuvius, the sides of the mountain are deeply scarred by lava flows, but its fertile lower slopes are dotted with villages and covered with rich volcanic soil.

'Give me a condor's quill! Give me Vesuvius' crater for an inkstand!'

Herman Melville

Lava flowing down a volcano can resemble a sluggish river; here it's a wave crashing on the shore, or some pyrotechnic

ballet dancing on rocks in their inert state – a reminder that our fragile world depends upon the planet's good behaviour

EARTH'S DEADLIEST ERUPTION

Mount Tambora
Location: Indonesia
Coordinates: 08° 14′ 00″ N | 117° 55′ 00″ W

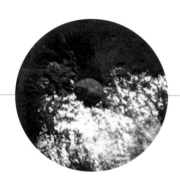

Between April 12 and 14, 1815, 60,000 people died from the multiple eruptions of Mount Tambora, and an additional 82,000 died of famine and disease brought on by the explosion. Around the world, 1815 came to be known as the "year without a summer" because all the ash, heavy, volcanic glass, rock flakes, and toxic gases darkened the sky, thereby dropping the temperature several degrees. In the United States, the New England states had killing frosts in July and August.

Another famous Indonesian eruption became history's second deadliest: between April 26 and 28, 1883, a 20-hour, 56-minute series of huge blasts ripped through the island of Krakatoa. The explosion was so loud that people 4,800 kilometres away heard the blast, which had the equivalent power of 223 million tonnes of TNT. Krakatoa ejected so much dust into the air that sunsets around the world were tinged red for two years afterwards.

Estimates suggest that Krakatoa shot material as high as 48 kilometres into the stratosphere, which in turn covered ships within a 3,200-kilometre radius with dust for weeks after the eruption. Debris was scattered across the Indian Ocean as far as Madagascar, and the outpouring of ash and lava was so great that new islands were formed around Krakatoa.

Pyroclastic flows on the first day of Krakatoa's eruption caused at least 2,000 human deaths. On the following day, the volcano's peak collapsed 305 metres below sea level, submerging the island and killing another 3,000 people. This collapse triggered a 37-metre-high tsunami that drowned more than 31,000 people as it crashed over the Indonesian islands of Java and Sumatra. Forty years later, in 1928, more eruptions gave birth to the Anak Krakatau, Rakata, Rakata Kecil, and Sertung islands.

After the earth-shattering explosion of Krakatoa in 1883, smaller eruptions have been grumbling away in the Sundra Strait since 1927, gradually forming new volcanic islands. Anak Krakatau, or 'the child of Krakatoa', was 44 years in the making. It now measures some 2 km across and is said to erupt once every 20 minutes.

EARTH'S DEADLIEST VOLCANIC ERUPTIONS OF THE 20TH AND 21ST CENTURIES

Volcanic disasters of the 20th and 21st centuries haven't matched their predecessors. The deadliest eruption of the 20th century was the May 8, 1902, eruption of Mount Pelée on Martinique in the West Indies. This killed 29,500 people almost instantaneously as a result of a *nuée ardente*, an incandescent, high-velocity cloud of volcanic dust and superheated gases that travelled more than 16 kilometres at speeds of 160 kilometres per hour. Pelée erupted just one day after a massive eruption of Soufrière on nearby St. Vincent and deposited a thick layer of volcanic ash over a wide expanse of land, turning it into a wasteland. Second to this was the relatively small eruption on November 13, 1985, of Nevado del Ruiz in Colombia. This outburst melted about 10 percent of the volcano's ice cover and caused history's deadliest landslide, which smothered 18,000 people.

The 20th century's largest volcanic eruption took place at Novarupta, on the Alaska Peninsula, on June 6-9, 1912. Lasting more than 60 hours, this eruption spewed 30 cubic kilometres of ash across the surrounding area. Although this eruption killed no one (thanks to effective evacuation), several villages along Alaska's south-east coast were buried, and more than a metre of volcanic ash collapsed rooftops in the town of Kodiak, more than 160 kilometres from the eruption's centre. The ash clogged rivers and streams, devastated the local fishing industry, choked vegetation, and blinded birds, bears, and other animals.

'When the sulfur and chlorine gases pouring out of these (volcanic) vents mix with the rainy climate, they form hydrochloric acid and hydrosulfuric acid which are very corrosive. The first day the TV crew lost seven cameras from exposure to the air... The acid even ate my eyeglasses. But because this relatively strong acid occurs in the form of rain, you get really clean. It eats the top layer off your skin.'

Writer Donovan Webster, atop Ambrym volcano, South Pacific

EARTH'S DEADLIEST VOLCANIC ERUPTIONS IN RECORDED HISTORY

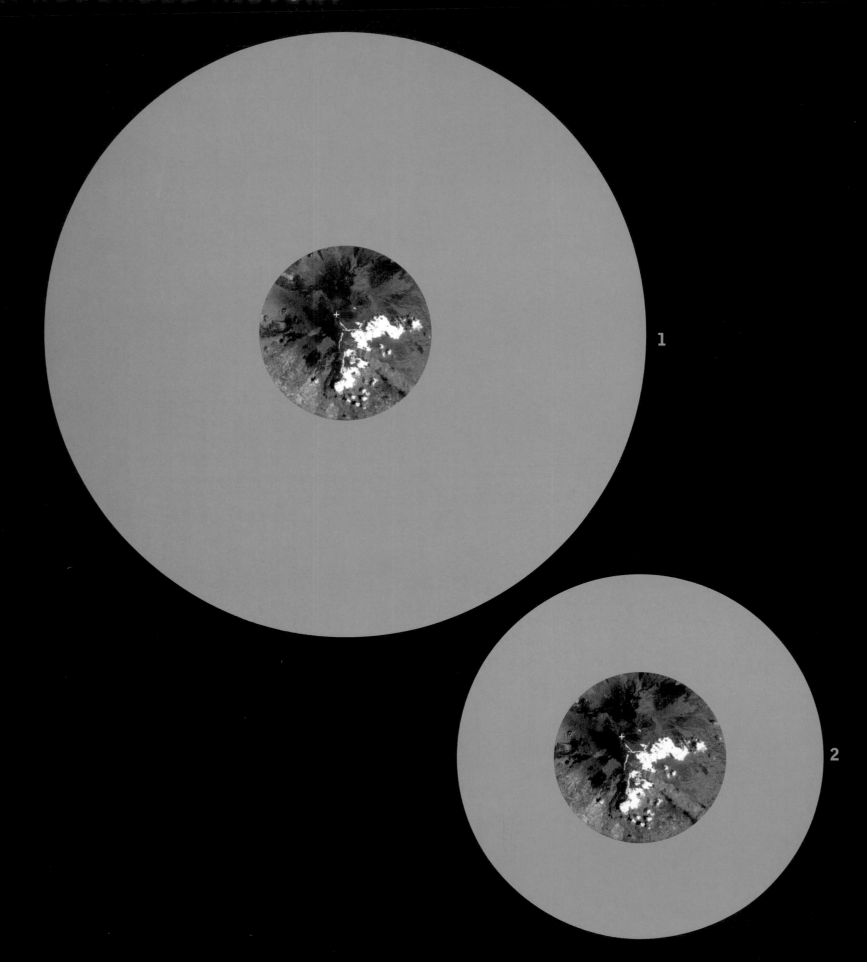

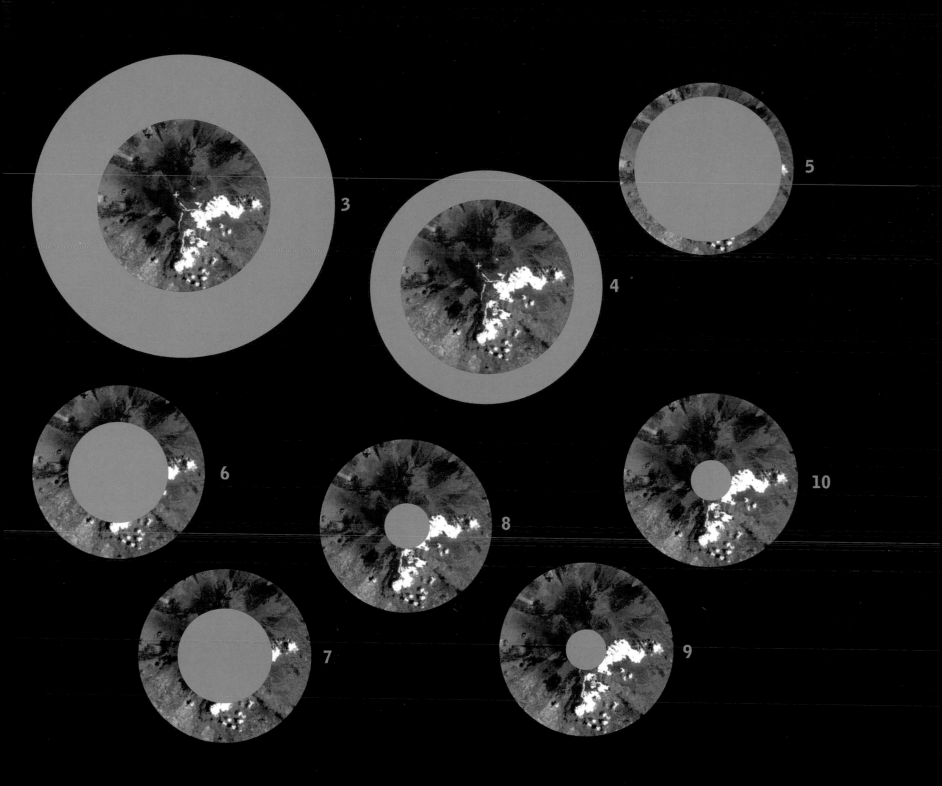

1 TAMBORO, INDONESIA | 1815 | DEATHS: 60,000 | CAUSE: FAMINE AND DISEASE
2 KRAKATOA, INDONESIA | 1883 | DEATHS: 36,417 | CAUSE: TSUNAMI
3 PELÉE, MARTINIQUE | 1902 | DEATHS: 29,500 | CAUSE: ASHFLOW
4 NEVADO DEL RUIZ, COLOMBIA | 1985 | DEATHS: 23,080 | CAUSE: MUDFLOWS
5 UNZEN, JAPAN | 1792 | DEATHS: 14,524 | CAUSE: TSUNAMI
6 KELUT, INDONESIA | 1586 | DEATHS: 10,000 | CAUSE: MUDFLOWS AND ASHFLOWS
7 LAKI, ICELAND | 1783 | DEATHS: 9,350 | CAUSE: STARVATION
8 SANTA MARIA, GUATEMALA | 1902 | DEATHS: 4,500 | CAUSE: DISEASE
9 GALUNGGUNG, INDONESIA | 1882 | DEATHS: 4,011 | CAUSE: ASHFLOWS
10 VESUVIUS, ITALY | 1631 | DEATHS: 4,000 | CAUSE: ASHFLOWS

EARTH'S LARGEST LAVA TREE GROVE

Kilauea
Location: Island of Hawaii ("Big Island"), Hawaii, U.S.A.
Coordinates: 19° 24' 00" N | 155° 17' 00" W

Lava trees are created when hot lava congeals around a tree trunk containing water. Lava overtakes a tree and boils the water inside it, which then turns to steam and cools the lava, solidifying it before the tree burns entirely. The world's largest lava-tree grove is at Lava Tree State Monument, in the Nanawale Forest Reserve, at a site where a lava flow burned through a grove of ohia trees in 1790. The lava poured out from Kilauea's east rift zone, surrounded the trees, and eventually cooled, forming moulds of the burning tree trunks.

Lava trees, or petrified stumps of what were once vital trees, have the appearance of introspective druids, wandering the forest, searching for some lost remedy that might bring them back to life. This park has a ghostly quality, not unlike the ashen moulds of Pompeians, who were fixed in time by the sudden, dense ash plumes of Vesuvius erupting in 79 C.E. Lava trees, however, are hardly the only fantastic sight in east Hawaii. Not far away, in Pahoa, is a formation called "Pele's Hair". Pele is the Hawaiian goddess of fire, and her "hair" is composed of long, fragile strands of solidified lava crystal that resemble flowing locks.

EARTH'S MOST VARIED VOLCANIC MASSIF

Tongariro
Location: New Zealand's North Island
Coordinates: 39° 17' 27" S | 175° 33' 44" E

The multicoloured, lunar-like volcanic massif of Tongariro, on New Zealand's North Island, is both otherworldly and spectacular. A toxic, turquoise mountain lake surrounded by decaying, sand-hued decaying mounds, the Tongariro massif comprises several volcanic cones, rising to a peak elevation of 1,968 metres. The centre is surrounded by an extensive ring plain made of stream, debris flow, lahar, lava, and ashflow deposits. As a result, the land combines remarkable contrasts of barren lava flows, winter snowfields, hot springs, and active craters. The varied vegetation looks prehistoric; no one quite understands how it manages to eke out an existence on the poor pumice soil.

Tongariro is New Zealand's first national park, a World Heritage site, and a cultural and religious hub for the local Maori people. One creation myth holds that a Maori ancestor, Ngatoroirangi, was near death after exploring this mountainous region. He called out to his sisters from his Pacific homeland, Hawaiiki, to send him fire. The fire was delivered, and its flaming passage left a trail of volcanic vents across this amazing massif.

Tongariro is a complex formed from more than a dozen composite cones. The youngest, Ngauruhoe, has grown into the high point of the massif since its birth some 2,500 years ago, while steep-sided Ngauruhoe and its neighbour, Ruapehu, have fumed and fulminated away to become New Zealand's most active volcanoes in historical memory.

EARTH'S MOST VOLCANIC ZONE

Ring of Fire encircling the Pacific Ocean
Range of coordinates

This fiery loop – truly a ring of fire – of more than 300 volcanoes circles much of the Pacific Ocean, from the South Pacific islands to Indonesia, Japan, Alaska, north-west America, Mexico, Central America, and South America. It marks the boundary of one of the world's first tectonic plates and contains more than half the world's active volcanoes (above sea level). The zone is notorious for frequent earthquakes and volcanic eruptions. At the very heart of the ring, in the middle of the Pacific Ocean, is the Hawaiian "hot spot", home to some of Earth's most active volcanoes. A hot spot is an intensely hot region deep within the earth. Frequently, a fissure opens in one of these spots and molten rock seeps out and rises towards the ocean's surface. The Ring of Fire isn't the world's only underwater volcanically active region; another occurs along a rift zone underneath Iceland.

Alchemists believed that fire and water were opposing elements – a credo that still holds true in the Pacific where Sulawesi (above) erupts in Indonesia. The seismic instability of its volcanic 'ring of fire' also unleashes the power of tsunami. Earthquakes and eruptions repulse the water and the giant waves wreak havoc thousands of miles away.

Mount St. Helens with a noble brow of white snow at left; on the opposite page, Mount St. Helens a headless,
burned-out ruin, having spewed her molten guts all over, flinging vast quantities of rock and hurling volcanic ash up to
the stratosphere. Before she blew, scientists observed the mountain bulging with magma and steam. Few eruptions of

recent times have demonstrated so clearly the titanic forces of pressure and heat that build up deep within the earth, cooking away until something on the surface has to give. This almost literal decapitation of a mountain reminds us that landscapes we have known and loved all our lives — the very contours of our world — can change almost overnight.

The island of Java is studded with snow-capped volcanoes, rising like conical white clouds above flat green paddies and lacy palms. The temple at Borobodur, one of the wonders of the Buddhist world, is encircled by volcanic peaks, their solemn forms echoed in the stone stupas laid out all around the temple mandala. One of Java's most revered

and beautiful volcanoes is Mount Bromo (above) on the island's eastern side. The name derives from Betara Bromo, god of fire, who sprang from a different cosmology. And every year, to this day, people of the Kejawen sects – a mix of Java's aboriginal religion and Islam – offer fruit, vegetables, rice and meat to please their native mountain deity.

4

WA

'All of a sudden there came a great noise and we saw a great black thing a long way off, coming towards us. It was very high and very strong, and we soon saw that it was water. Within seconds trees and houses were washed away. Not far off was some steep sloping ground. We ran towards it and tried to climb up out of the way of the water but the wave was too quick for most of them. Those below tried to make those above them move on by biting their heels, but they could not let go their death grip. A great struggle took place for a few moments, but one after another, they were washed down and carried far away by the rushing waters. You can still see the marks on the hillside where the fight for life took place.'

A. Scarth, a Javanese farmworker who lived through the 1999 tsunami in Lampong Bay, Indonesia

EARTH'S MOST POWERFUL TSUNAMIS

TALLEST: Lituya Bay, Alaska, U.S.A. (1958): 58° 38′ 13″ N | 137° 34′ 23″ W

FASTEST: Hilo, Hawaii, U.S.A. (1946): 19° 43′ 47″ N | 155° 05′ 24″ W

DEADLIEST: Krakatoa, Indonesia (1883): 06° 07′ 00″ S | 105° 24′ 00″ E

The infamous eruption of Krakatoa in 1883 may have been history's second-deadliest volcanic eruption, but only about 5,000 of the total number of 36,000 human deaths were caused by lava, ash, pyroclastic flows, and the collapse of the volcano. Rather, it was the 37-metre-high tsunami, triggered by the mountain's collapse – which swept over the Indonesian islands of Java and Sumatra and whose effects were felt as far away as France – that was the major killer.

Tsunamis are a series of sea waves caused by a massive shift of the seafloor during an earthquake or volcanic eruption. The waves radiate from the site of the disturbance in widening circles and can travel great distances at speeds faster than 800 kilometres per hour. In the Pacific Ocean, a tsunami can course through water five kilometres deep yet create waves only a metre tall. But when they hit shallow areas along seacoasts, these waves pile up into walls of water that can be more than 30 metres high. Measurements of the tallest recorded tsunami are in dispute: according to the U.S. Navy Meteorology and Oceanography Command, history's tallest tsunami reached 64 metres – the height of an 18-story building – when it reached Siberia's Kamchatka Peninsula in 1737. But a substantially larger tsunami was triggered on July 9, 1958, by massive landslides at the head of Lituya Bay on the southern coast of Alaska. With a terrifying height of 524 metres, this is the biggest superwave ever measured.

The world's fastest-moving tsunami was triggered by an earthquake in Alaska and travelled at more than 700 km per hour to strike Hilo, Hawaii, on April 1, 1946. Another broke over the city in 1960, prompting the authorities to build an 8-m hill for protection. Scientists have recently begun to explore a still more devastating incarnation of these giant waves, the so-called mega-tsunami, precipitated by massive landslips into the sea.

Ellen MacArthur

OCEAN

No matter how many years I spend on the oceans I will only understand a fraction of their beauty and power. The oceans cover three-quarters of the earth's surface, and their depths remain one of the few unexplored areas of the planet. Consider: the Marianas Trench, which sinks 10 kilometres below the ocean's surface, is the deepest place on earth – deeper than Mount Everest is tall.

From the Bermuda Triangle to the mystery-filled waters between the mythical rock at the tip of South America and the Antarctic peninsula, the oceans are among the most diverse environments. Each feels like a different planet, with its own landscape, temperament and light, not to mention colours: the azure blue and turquoise green of the Caribbean, the inky black of the Gulf Stream, the grey of the Southern Ocean, which is wonderfully interrupted by the odd bright-blue flash. Here, the waves are almost always followed by swelling breakers that foam at their peaks but then go strangely calm as they disappear, leaving a blanket of white in their wake.

Nor can I anticipate the sea's movements. Experience has taught me only to predict them with a bit more accuracy, and to understand what conditions may prevail in a storm. It has also taught me that the winds above the ocean are primarily responsible for the changing mood of the water below. And while oceans can be frightening and unpredictable, it's in large part because they're always reacting to the weather that passes over them, or the land that defines their boundaries.

Weather has not been on our side lately. It's been testing us, pushing us hard. In the beginning of this trip we were confronted not with gales and storms, but with complete stillness, which can be more maddening. Then, after a week, we got caught in the tail end of Hurricane Bertha, which had swept up the east coast of North America from the Florida Keys towards Newport, Rhode Island.

This was my first real storm at sea. The clear skies disappeared behind a solid black cloud, the bright blue water changed to an ominous grey, and the last of the sun's golden warmth was etched away by the encroaching mass.

The storm hit and lasted more than two days. I was gripped by the size and power of the waves. The boat would regularly fall off the waves, slamming into them, sending a shudder through her entire 18-metre body. When I was at the helm I felt myself stepping up a gear, speeding along, trying to carve a path though the swells. I reached a surfing speed of 19.54 knots – my fastest ever – as much a result of the force of the big swells as the 40 knots of wind power urging us along.

At the helm, I searched for the troughs that would get the best surf speeds. As she rolled, the idle slabs of main sail hanging under the boom lit up like a theatre set. The bow wave grew and glowed, creating a suspense akin to the drop on a fairground ride. Then, as the bow fell, the vibration began and the boat sped off, as if jet-propelled. It seemed like an eternity before she caught the foot of the next trough ahead.

As she slowed, another large wave slewed her stern around. I summoned all of my strength – I had my feet jammed against the toe rail – and this time I really struggled to stop her. She heeled over, and again I found myself up to my knees in water (Yes, Mum, I was clipped on).

At 0430, I handed the helm over to Alan, my only companion for hundreds of miles. I stayed up for another 15 minutes, then went below to empty my boots. My feet were soaked and wet, my legs aching with cold.

People rarely believe me when I tell them that one of the greatest dangers of the sea is the land itself. The sea grows angrier as the land beneath it shallows; it turns more violent when its freedom to move is restricted. You can see this from land when the waves crash against rocks or beaches. I think of it as the wild sea's response to being hemmed in. It's not unlike the difference between wandering the moors and being trapped on a London tube train.

The sea should never be underestimated or disrespected. If I ever find myself feeling complacent about it, I know I'll have to give up sailing, for there will be no rightful place for me on the earth's waters.

EARTH'S LARGEST SUBMARINE SINKHOLE

The Blue Hole
Location: Lighthouse Reef, Belize
Total Size: 300 m across | roughly 137 m deep
Coordinates: 17° 15′ 00″ N | 87° 30′ 00″ W

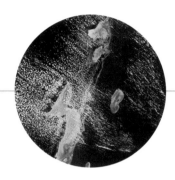

Seen from above, the Blue Hole looks like Earth's all-seeing eye: an indigo iris surrounded by an emerald sea. The secret behind (or beneath) this remarkable formation is *karst*. *Karst* is an area of land with a soft limestone foundation that is honeycombed with sinkholes, underground streams, and caves. The term comes from the Karst region of Yugoslavia, which is rugged and riddled with innumerable caves. Half a world away, in the Caribbean Sea, 80 kilometres off the coast of Belize, lies the world's most spectacular example of karst: the Blue Hole.

The Blue Hole was formed 15,000 years ago when glaciers covered much of Europe and North America. With the decline of the Ice Age and the rise of sea levels, many karstified cave systems flooded and, over time, collapsed. On land, some formed minor depressions or holes in the ground. But others created something more spectacular. The Blue Hole is the result of a huge cavern's collapse. It was first explored by Jacques Cousteau in 1970 and has since become a diver's pilgrimage site. Although the sinkhole is best seen from an aeroplane, divers compare the experience of dipping below the shallow lip to explore a cavern filled with stalactites and stalagmites to swimming down a mine shaft. It's the thrill that explains the luggage stickers that say, "I dived the Blue Hole."

EARTH'S LONGEST REEF AND LARGEST CORAL DOMAIN

The Great Barrier Reef
Location: Australia's north-east coast
Total Size: 2,012 km long | 350,000 km² total area
Coordinates: 18° 00′ 00″ S | 146° 50′ 00″ E

It's not the "world's largest living creature", as some have termed it. But the rainbow-coloured coral shelves that stretch across Australia's north-eastern coast are alive in countless respects.

Although its name suggests a single strip of land, the Great Barrier Reef is a commonwealth of some 2,100 individual reefs and 800 fringing reefs built over millions of years from the skeletons of living marine organisms. The building blocks of the reef structure are formed by the remains of tiny creatures known as *coral polyps* and *hydrocorals*, while the glue that binds them together is constructed mainly of algae and microscopic plants. Washing over it are clear waters ranging in temperature from 21°C to 38°C and an enormous diversity of aquatic plants and animals: anemones, jellyfish, sponges, worms, gastropods, lobsters, crayfish, prawns, crabs, more

than 2,000 species of fish, 4,000 species of mollusc, and six of the world's seven species of sea turtle.

Unfortunately, the predators of this reef are not limited to the whitetip sharks patrolling its nooks and crannies. Overfishing, invasive species, efforts to mine and drill for petroleum resources, coral collectors, and overzealous tourism continue to threaten this underwater ecosystem. One major concern is coral bleaching, in which corals lose their symbiotic algae and turn white; unusually hot water is the culprit, but heat in this instance is relative. Even a slight increase in temperature from, say, global warming, can spell doom. The variety and vibrancy of this coral domain are unrivalled anywhere on Earth. How long we will able to enjoy it is in large part for us to determine.

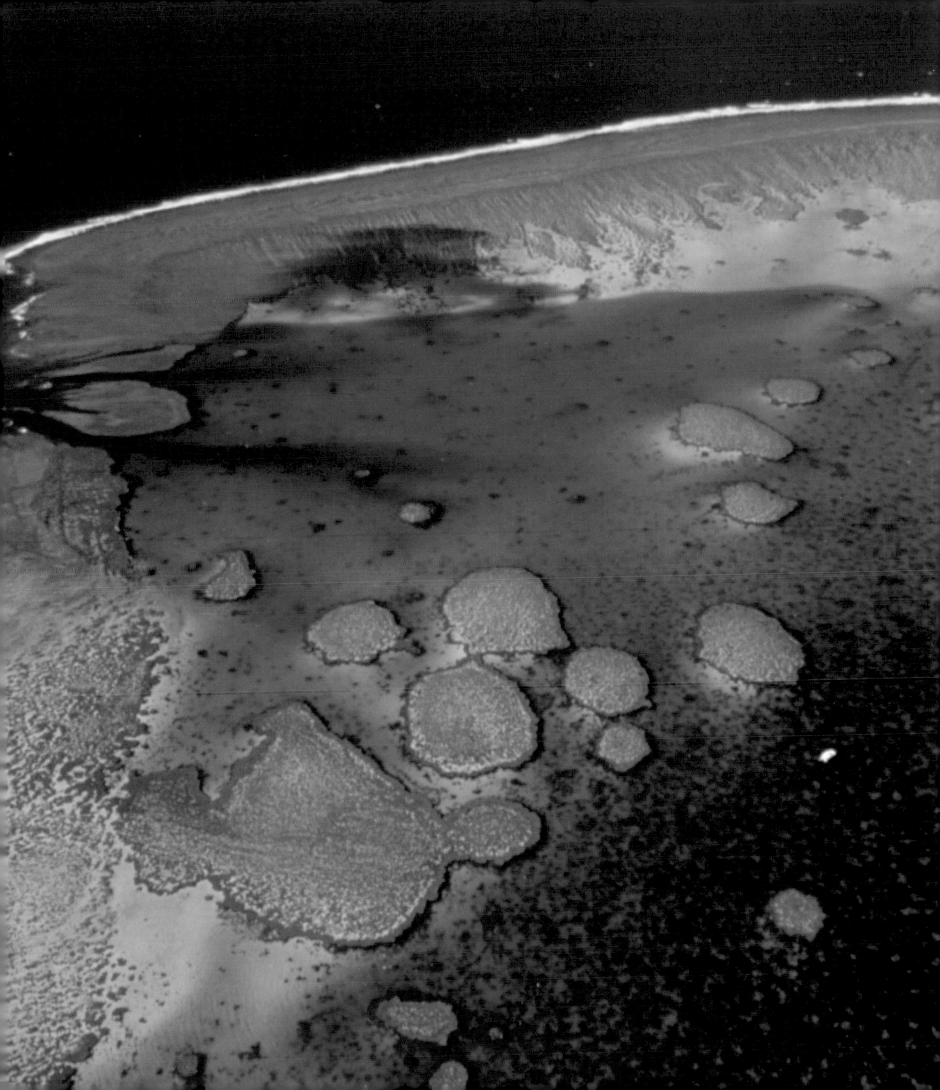

EARTH'S BIGGEST ATOLL

Kiritimati
Location: Eastern Kiribati, South Pacific
Coordinates: 01° 52′ 00″ N | 157° 25′ 00″ W

Kiritimati, also known as Christmas Island, is the world's largest atoll, with a total land area of 575 square kilometres and a population of fewer than 3,000. Its history is marked by industry and infamy. In 1777, it was famously explored by Captain James Cook. More ominously, nuclear bombs were exploded on the atoll in 1957 and 1958 by the British and, in 1962, the Americans.

Atolls form when a volcano erupts on the ocean floor, piling up lava that over time breaks through the ocean's surface and creates an island. Just below the waterline, corals begin to build a limestone reef, which grows over millions of years even while the volcano beneath it is sinking. Waves eventually break down the ring-shaped reef, piling sand on the remaining coral to create an island. The world's largest raised coral atoll is Lifou (Lifu) in the Loyalty Islands of New Caledonia, which measures 1,146 square kilometres. The people of Kiritimati are mainly Micronesian, with a small group of Polynesians from Tuvalu, and other expatriates. Copra plantations thrive, and fishing is prevalent. Some islanders claim never to have left their floating world, and there are good reasons to stay: long beaches of coral sand dotted with coconut palms, and lush villages with the names of far-off places, like London, Poland, Paris, and – breaking the tradition – Banana.

'Coral is set budding under seas,
Though none, O none sees what patterns it is making?'

Philip Larkin

EARTH'S FASTEST-SINKING ISLANDS

Maldives Republic
Location: North Indian Ocean
Coordinates: 03° 12′ 00″ N | 73° 00′ 00″ E

Oceans cover almost three-quarters of our planet's surface. The remaining 29 percent – land above sea level – is all we have to cling to, and global warming is reducing this minority share even further by melting ice caps, which will in turn raise sea levels and flood low-lying coastal land. Because all oceans are rising at a consistent rate of about 2 to 4 centimetres annually, or about a metre every 20 years, Earth's lowest-lying islands will most likely disappear within the next half-century. Sinking most prominently is the Maldives, the world's lowest island nation. Comprising 1,192 coral isles in the Indian Ocean, the country's territory covers 90,000 square kilometres, 99 percent of which is water. Its highest island, Wilingili, has a peak elevation of only 2.4 metres above sea level, so even a tiny rise in the ocean level would leave it vulnerable to even mid-size storm surges and tidal waves.

The Pacific is dotted with more than 25,000 islands, many of them sinking. Takuu, an island in Papua, New Guinea, will likely be the first to go; plans are now being made to relocate its 2,500 inhabitants. If the isolated Melanesians of Takuu are forced to resettle on a different island, their unique civilization will face great strain. Indigenous Takuu islanders record and share their history through song; it's not uncommon for a local to be able to sing a thousand songs from memory. If their home is washed away, their traditions will go along with it.

Tuvalu, a string of nine coral atolls 5 m above sea level at their highest point, could sink in the next half-century. Other threatened Pacific islands include Kiribati, Niue, and the Marshall Islands. Even Bangladesh and Sri Lanka are already feeling the effects of sea erosion and warmer waters, which are effectively poisoning coral and marine life.

EARTH'S LARGEST OCEAN

Pacific Ocean
Total Size: About 696,000,000 km³ of water
No geographic coordinates

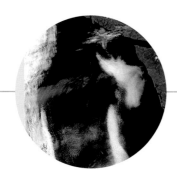

About 71 percent of the earth's surface is covered by water, and roughly one-third of that is covered by the Pacific Ocean, which at its widest point stretches nearly halfway around the globe. This enormous body contains 46 percent of the earth's water – more than all the world's other seas and oceans combined

The Pacific Ocean contains the planet's lowest point – Challenger Deep, 10,911 metres down in the Mariana Trench – and a massive portion of the world's longest mountain range, the Mid-Oceanic Ridge, which circumnavigates the globe underwater. What is happening beneath the surface is arguably more interesting than what is happening above it. This is where massive plates are converging and pulling apart in a tectonic dance that unleashes the earth's magma and gives rise to seamounts and volcanic islands.

Exploration of the Pacific perhaps began with the early Asians who sailed to distant islands in primitive boats. In the 15th century, the Italian traveller Marco Polo brought home news of a "new" ocean off Asia. The Spanish explorer Vasco Nuñez de Balboa confirmed the Pacific as distinct from the Atlantic, and his countryman Ferdinand Magellan mistakenly named the ocean – which can produce violent tides and storms – in honour of its calm waters (*pacifica* means tranquil).

With its tsunamis and 'ring of fire', the name Pacific, or 'peaceful', is a misnomer of dimensions almost as spectacular as those of the ocean itself.

EARTH'S SMALLEST OCEAN

Arctic Ocean
Location: North Pole
Total Size: 14,000,000 km²
Coordinates: 85° 00′ 00″ N | 00° 00′ 00″ W

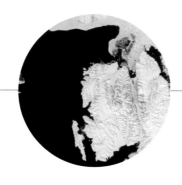

Though it's the smallest and shallowest of the world's four oceans (after the Pacific, Atlantic, and Indian), the Arctic Ocean illustrates the relative land-to-water proportions on Earth. Including its bays and seas, the Arctic Ocean is 1.5 times larger than the United States, yet it constitutes only 4 percent of the world's oceans. Thirteen Arctic Oceans could fit into the Pacific basin.

From October to June the Arctic Ocean is virtually covered by an expansive polar ice pack; in summer this shrinks by half. Although it was once thought that no nonoceanic life could exist in a terrain of ice floes and freezing temperatures — they frequently plummet to -50°C in winter — some animals, such as polar bears, seals, and gulls, thrive here. The winters bring perpetual darkness

and clear skies, while summers deliver continuous daylight and a damp, foggy mist.

The Inuit term for any mountain peak that pokes through the ice blanket is "nunatak". Earth's northernmost nunatak, or point of land, is often considered to be Oodaaq Island, which was discovered in 1900 by Robert Peary. But this strip of gravel, 1,600 kilometres north of the Arctic Circle, is sometimes covered by ice and hard to find. Global warming could reveal more of Oodaaq Island in the future, but at a high cost.

Already, a thinning polar ice pack threatens the Arctic Ocean, which is home to endangered walruses and whales. Despite the tough appearance of Arctic ice, this ecosystem is seriously vulnerable to change and damage.

Excluding its fringe areas, the Arctic Ocean is covered with drifting sea ice throughout the year. In contrast to Antarctica, which is a land continent bounded by oceans, the Arctic mass is almost all water and ice.

EARTH'S LARGEST SEA

South China Sea
Location: Between the South-east Asian mainland and Taiwan, the Philippines, and Malaysia
Total Size: 2,590,600 km²
Coordinates: 15° 00′ 00″ N | 115° 00′ 00″ E

Bordered by some of the world's most rapidly industrializing countries and traversed by some of the world's busiest shipping lanes – half the world's supertankers pass through this region's waters – the South China Sea is now more vital than ever. Spanning an area between mainland South-east Asia and the islands of Taiwan, the Philippines, Malaysia, and Indonesia, the South China Sea is dotted with hundreds of islets, reefs, rocks and shoals, which are the subject of conflicting territorial claims.

Some geographers question whether the Coral Sea – the south-western arm of the Pacific Ocean, extending east of Australia and New Guinea – shouldn't claim the title of the world's biggest. In total, it covers an area of 4,791,000 square kilometres and is distinguished by the Great Barrier Reef, which extends over 2,000 kilometres down Australia's north-east coast. But most geographic records incorporate the Coral Sea into the Pacific Ocean, and the immense Arabian Sea shares this same fate; thus, South China is left as the world's largest sea.

The South China Sea supports a diverse ecosystem due to its boundaries of archipelagoes and peninsulas, dotted by small islands and coral reefs. Extensive coral reefs support several thousand species of organisms and play a central role in reducing erosion from the impact of waves on beaches.

EARTH'S OCEANS

1 PACIFIC OCEAN | AREA: 180,000,000 km² | AVERAGE DEPTH: 4,300 m
2 ATLANTIC OCEAN | AREA: 82,362,000 km² | AVERAGE DEPTH: 3,658 m
3 INDIAN OCEAN | AREA: 73,426,500 km² | AVERAGE DEPTH: 3,353 m
4 ARCTIC OCEAN | AREA: 14,000,000 km² | AVERAGE DEPTH: 3,700 m

Measurements are correct according to the Columbia Gazetteer of the World and the Merriam Webster Geographical Dictionary. Place names verified through the United States Board on Geographic Names and the National Imagery Mapping Agency's (NIMA) geographic names database.

EARTH'S LONGEST RIVER

Nile
Location: Central and North Africa
Total Length: 6,695 km
Coordinates: 30° 10' 00" N | 31° 06' 00" E

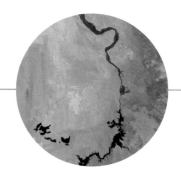

It begins as a tiny trickle high in the forested mountains above Africa's Great Rift Valley, but grows as it meanders over cataracts and through shallow lakes, winding across the desert on its way to the Mediterranean Sea. The north-flowing Nile drains 2,850,000 square kilometres of land, and its waters support 98 percent of all agriculture in Egypt.

The Nile is best known historically as the lifeline of one of the world's earliest civilizations, that of the ancient Egyptians, who settled on these fertile banks (flooded each year with silt from Ethiopia's highlands) 5,000 years ago. Without the Nile and its floodplain, Egypt's prospects would have been smothered by the Sahara. But with the Nile's waters and rich sediment, Egyptian farmers were able both to harvest crops and to transport them. Papyrus reeds growing in the water became

paper for writing, and lucrative trading routes along the Nile led to the construction of cities, temples, and tombs for kings and pharaohs. The Egyptians became one of the world's most technically accomplished civilizations, and they left behind architecture and art of eternal significance.

Ever since Ptolemy held that the great river's origin was the "mountains of the moon", the source of the Nile has been a challenge for explorers. For a long time, it was believed that its source was Lake Victoria, the world's second-largest freshwater lake. It wasn't until 1937 that a German explorer, Burkhart Waldecker, located the elusive trickle (in the mountains of modern-day Burundi) that feeds Lake Victoria, which in turn gives rise to the Nile.

'He who rides the sea of the Nile must have sails woven of patience.'

William Golding

EARTH'S MOST DEADLY FLOOD

Hwang Ho (Yellow River), 1931
Location: China
Coordinates: 37° 45′ 27″ N | 119° 04′ 34″ E

China's Yangtze River gets all the attention. It is, after all, the world's third-longest river (more than 5,552 kilometres), and one-third of China's population lives along its banks and in adjacent regions. Because of its high flood risk – in the 2,100 years between the early Han dynasty and the late Qing dynasty, the Yangzte flooded an average of once every 10 years, claiming tens of thousands of lives – China has undertaken the greatest construction project since the Great Wall. When it is completed in 2009, the Three Gorges Dam will be the world's largest hydropower station and dam, with a 2-kilometre stretch of concrete and a 595-kilometre-long reservoir.

But the Yangtze, even with its annual flooding – which raises water levels 6 to 17 metres higher – is not responsible for history's worst flood. Instead, it is China's Hwang Ho (Yellow River) that has, over the centuries, been the most murderous. This 4,828-kilometre-long river, which originates in the northern mountain province of Qinghai and ends at the Yellow Sea, killed nearly 2 million people in 1887 and almost 1 million in 1938. In August 1931, an overflow known as "China's Sorrow" left more than 3.7 million people dead from flooding and subsequent starvation. Millions more were left homeless.

Silt deposited by the Hwang Ho created the immense, alluvial North China Plain, one of the nation's important agricultural regions. But the river's millions of tonnes of silt can cause it to overflow. The Chinese have tried to control the Yellow River by building dikes, dams, and channels, but it will take the success of the massive Xiaolangdi Multipurpose Dam Project to stop the devastation.

How are the mighty fallen. In 1972, the once-fearsome Yellow River (shown frozen above) failed to reach the sea in the dry season for the first time in history. By 1998, the lakes on the Tibetan plateau feeding the headwaters had halved to 2,000, with 4,500 diversion projects siphoning off what strength remained in this erstwhile dragon of a river.

EARTH'S MOST VOLUMINOUS RIVER

Amazon River
Location: Brazil, South America
Coordinates: 00° 10' 00" S | 49° 00' 00" W

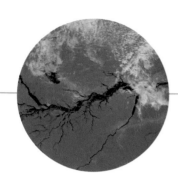

Vast, rich, and threatened, the Amazon is South America's greatest river by volume and the world's largest drainage system. Second in length only to the Nile, the 6,270-kilometre-long Amazon sustains the world's largest rain forest – about half the earth's remaining rain forest – and its greatest diversity of flora and fauna. The waters of the Amazon support at least 1,500 species of fish (compare this with Europe, which has only about 150 fish species) and nearly three-quarters of the world's known plant species.

Metaphor mingles with science in the Amazon. One creation myth holds that the river was born of the doomed romance between the moon and the sun. Unable to share the skies simultaneously with her beloved sun, the moon wept, her tears filling the forest and running into the sea. The great river was named in 1541 by Spanish explorer Francisco de Orellana in honour of the female warriors of Greek mythology, as he reported battling tribes of bellicose women

protecting its banks.

The Amazon's source is in the high Andes of Peru, 160 kilometres from the Pacific Ocean, and its delta is on the other side of the continent, a 240-kilometre-wide estuary at the Atlantic coast, studded with low muddy islands. The waterway carries more liquid than the world's next 10 biggest rivers combined, roughly one-fifth of all the water that runs off Earth's surface. It discharges about 6.5 cubic kilometres of water a minute into the Atlantic Ocean, enough for everyone in the world to have an 80-litre bath every 40 minutes. This flow is so powerful that it dilutes ocean water 160 kilometres beyond the coastline.

The Amazon River is home to wildlife (such as electric eels, hummingbirds, parrots, anacondas, alligators, and giant butterflies) as well as cultural traditions and folklore practised by some of the indigenous groups (like the Panara tribe and the Yanomami people) that have inhabited this majestic ecosystem for millennia.

EARTH'S WIDEST WATERFALL

Iguazú Falls
Location: Argentina-Brazil border
Coordinates: 25° 41′ 00″ S | 54° 26′ 00″ W

The roar of Iguazú Falls can be heard long before its cascades come into view. Far away, the furious current of the 1,320-kilometre-long Iguazú River, which forms the border between Brazil and Argentina, announces a torrent of water that in a heavy rainy season swells to twice the volume of water spilling over Niagara Falls (in the dry season, however, this cascade can fade to a mere silent mist).

Strung out along the rim of a 4-kilometre-long crescent-shaped cliff is a series of some 275 individual cascades and waterfalls separated by rocky, densely wooded islets. Some of the cascades plummet straight down, 82 metres into the Devil's Throat gorge below. Others are interrupted by ledges and send up clouds of mist and spray, creating a dazzling hazy rainbow display. This spectacular falling-water network rests on a lava plateau that was pushed up to Earth's surface more than 135 million years ago. Surrounding the falls are luxuriant forests, filled with bamboo, palms, and delicate tree ferns; parrots and macaws flit through the foliage, competing for attention with exotic wild orchids, begonias, and bromeliads.

In the local Indian language, the name Iguazú simply means "great waters"; early civilizations considered it to be "the place where clouds are born". According to legend, the great waterfall was created in an outburst of rage by the god of the Iguazú River, who lived in a particularly wild and violent area of the downpour called the Garganta do Diablo (Devil's Throat).

The first European to see the falls was the Spanish explorer Alvar Nuñes in 1541, who noted in his journal that "the current of Iguazú was so strong that the canoes were carried furiously down the river ... the noise made by the water leaping down some high rocks into a chasm may be heard a great distance off, and the spray rises to two spear-throws and more above the fall."

Guarani Indian legend says that Iguazú Falls came into being when a forest god, infatuated with a young girl, blasted
the riverbed to stop a human rival from spiriting her away in his canoe. The girl plunged over a precipice and when she

reached the bottom, she turned into a rock, to be washed forever in the rolling thunder of the waters. Her lover survived in the form of a tree, clinging to the cliffs above, doomed to lean forever over the abyss searching for his lost love.

EARTH'S HIGHEST WATERFALL

Angel Falls
Location: Canaima, Venezuela
Total Height: 979 m
Coordinates: 05° 57′ 00″ N | 62° 30′ 00″ W

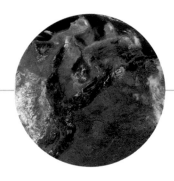

A popular pursuit in Depression-era America was plummeting in a wooden barrel over the 50-metre drop of Niagara Falls. Some daredevils even survived to collect a monetary reward.

Niagara Falls is a dripping kitchen tap compared with Venezuela's Angel Falls, the highest uninterrupted waterfall in the world. Although the longest drop on the falls is 807 metres – more than twice the height of the Eiffel Tower and higher than the Empire State Building in New York City – the overall height of Angel Falls is another 172 metres higher still. Because of this incredible drop, water disperses into a fine mist by the time it hits the ground.

The falls are named for (and by) the American Jimmy Angel, who in 1933 flew into the canyon of the remote Churún River prospecting for gold. The image of the falls transfixed him, and he returned in 1937, landed his Flamingo monoplane on a sandstone mesa near the falls, and explored the area.

Unfortunately, Angel's plane got stuck in a marsh, forcing him to hike for 11 days back to civilization. This unexpected expedition led him past the fantastic falls that now bear his name.

The best way to see the falls and the only practical way to get there is by aeroplane. The season is essential: in the dry season (January to May), the falls may be just a thin trickle, but in the rainy season (June to December) they are roaring.

'…a waterfall grows slower and more lightly suspended as it plunges down.'

Friedrich Nietzsche

EARTH'S LARGEST CONCENTRATION OF GEYSERS

Yellowstone National Park
Location: Parts of Wyoming, Idaho, and Montana, U.S.A.
Coordinates: 44° 46′ 00″ N | 110° 14′ 00″ W

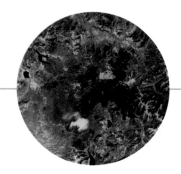

The world's best-known and most predictably exploding geyser is Wyoming's Old Faithful, in the United States' Yellowstone National Park, which erupts faithfully every 69 to 78 minutes.

Yellowstone lies on a volcanically active basin in the Rocky Mountains, ideal terrain for the mouth of a geyser, a tube hole filled with water that extends deep into the earth's crust. Magma near the bottom of such a hole heats the rocks surrounding the water, which in turn superheats the pressurized water above them. As the surface of this water begins to boil, pressure is released on the scalding water below, which turns to steam and erupts, ejecting a column of 93°C water upward. Evidence of the volcanic origins of the Yellowstone Plateau is in its nearly 10,000 thermal features, 300 geysers, and many vents and hot-mud pots. Old Faithful (right) gushes 21 to 23 times each day, shooting 41,640 litres of water about 46 metres high in each spurt. The world's highest-spouting geyser is Yellowstone's Steamboat Geyser, which sometimes reaches 122 metres!

Of course, Iceland — the world leader in all things geothermal — is responsible for naming spouting hot springs. With its first eruptions in the 14th century, Geysir (the Great Geyser, whose name means "gusher") fascinated locals and, although it is now extinct, lent its name to all successive shooting hot springs. Iceland still claims one of the world's most active geysers in Strokkur (the "butter churn"), which bubbles up and spouts on its own erratic schedule, about every 15 minutes.

EARTH'S BIGGEST ICEBERGS

Location: Antarctica and Greenland
No geographic coordinates

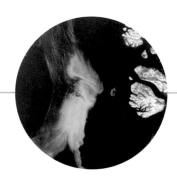

Icebergs are large chunks of freshwater ice that break off, or calve, from glaciers and float into the sea. The largest and tallest icebergs in recorded history disappeared decades ago, but their measurements remain uncontested. History's largest iceberg was sighted by the USS Glacier on November 12, 1956. It measured 335 kilometres long by 97 kilometres wide, roughly the size of Belgium. Less than one-eighth of an iceberg is visible above water.

Measured from top to bottom, history's tallest iceberg, discovered in 1958 off the coast of Greenland, rose 168 metres above the water's surface. For comparison, it was three times the height of the Leaning Tower of Pisa, though it is much more likely to topple.

In the Northern Hemisphere, most icebergs break off of glaciers from Greenland; sometimes they drift south on currents into the North Atlantic Ocean. The world's largest recent iceberg broke free from Antarctica's Ross Ice Shelf in early 2000. Satellite measurements by the U.S. National Oceanic and Atmospheric Administration determined the iceberg's dimensions to be 295 kilometres long and 37 kilometres wide, with a surface area about the size of Gambia or the Bahamas. Although global warming is causing ice sheets to melt, not all icebergs are the result of such warming. Some simply appear.

'Icebergs behoove the soul (both being self-made from elements least visible to see them so; fleshed, fair, erected indivisible.'

Elizabeth Bishop

Ice is intrinsically blue; red wavelengths in light are absorbed by the ice molecules, leaving blue light transmitted to the eyes. White results from air bubbles reflecting light by and from the reflection from the rough surface of bubbly ice.

'If the iceberg had recently fractured, its new face glistened greenish blue — the greens in the older, weathered faces were greyer. In twilight the ice took on the colours of the sun: rose, reddish yellows, watered purples,

soft pinks. The ice both reflected the light and trapped it within its crystalline corners and edges, where it intensified.' Barry Lopez, *Arctic Dreams*, 1986

EARTH'S LONGEST VALLEY GLACIER

Lambert-Fisher Glacier
Location: East Antarctica
Total Size: 515 km long | up to 65 km wide
Coordinates: 71° 00′ 00″ S | 70° 00′ 00″ E

A glacier is essentially a river of ice, a dense compaction of snow that spreads in all directions or moves slowly down a valley, carving a trench and picking up rock debris along the way. The Lambert-Fisher Glacier in East Antarctica is Earth's longest valley glacier, funnelling enormous amounts of ice from a major section of the East Antarctic plateau every year. This vast stretch covers an area of up to a million square kilometres, which makes it almost 10 times the size of Iceland. The Lambert Glacier moves between 400 and 900 metres per year, and as it spreads and thins, its speed can triple.

Antarctica's ice shelf is so heavy that it compresses and weighs down the land over much of the continent. The lowest point is the Bentley Subglacial Trench, 2,537 metres below sea level.

Although the Lambert Glacier is too frozen and remote to support a year-round scientific outpost, researchers have been studying and measuring it by satellite for clues to global climate change. For the last 10,000 years glaciers have been retreating, and most are melting faster than new ice is forming. One estimate is that if all the land ice melted, sea levels would rise approximately 70 metres worldwide. More realistically, even a slight melting of the polar ice caps could cause low-lying island groups, like the Maldives, to disappear beneath the ocean.

Antarctica's vast ice sheets may seem fundamentally hostile to life, but was it always so? Ten years ago, scientists found a stand of fossilized tree stumps 2,135 metres up on Mount Achernar, 800 kilometres north of the South Pole.

EARTH'S FASTEST-MOVING GLACIER

Columbia Glacier
Location: Alaska, between Anchorage and Valdez, U.S.A.
Coordinates: 61° 13′ 11″ N | 146° 53′ 43″ W

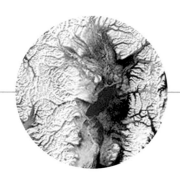

A galloping glacier – the term scientists use to describe a glacier that surges faster than the typical 2.5 to 5 centimetres per day – is a rare and destructive force. When a tranquil glacier starts to gallop, ice streams shutter, a wave of ice bulges to the front, the surface buckles, and creaky-cracking noises announce its advancement.

The world's fastest is currently the Columbia Glacier, which was calculated in 1999 to be flowing between Anchorage and Valdez in Alaska at an average rate of 35 metres per day.

Another mover and shaker is Kutiah Glacier, in the Karakoram Range west of the Himalaya, which in 1953 dashed more than 12 kilometres in three months, averaging 112 metres a day. Kutiah ploughed over forests and fields, and villages disappeared under its ice. Compared with most glaciers – such as the Athabasca Glacier in Canada's Rocky Mountains, which travels less than 1 metre a day – Kutiah's speed was nearly breakneck.

Scientists aren't sure why the Columbia Glacier is moving so quickly: its speed has almost doubled over the last 20 years. Some suggest that global warming has caused its ice to melt, loosen, and travel more quickly along the underlying bedrock down a slope.

The ground beneath glaciers is widened, gouged, and flattened as the ice flows downhill under the force of its own weight. But glaciers leave behind a beneficial wake, including billions of gallons of freshwater that feeds rivers, creates lakes, nourishes fertile soil, and produces spectacularly scenic mountain basins.

EARTH'S LONGEST FJORD

Nordvest Fjord
Location: Scoresbysund, eastern Greenland
Total Length: 314 km
Coordinates: 71° 40′ 00″ N | 27° 17′ 00″ W

In geological circles, there's a joke that goes like this: What do glaciers drive? Answer: Fjords. Fjords are long, narrow ocean inlets reaching far inland that form U-shaped valleys carved out by glaciers. A fjord's relatively calm surface belies its remarkable depth. A fjord is usually deepest farther inland, where the force of the glacier that formed it was greatest. Even though the inlet of a fjord can be comparatively shallow – reducing the exchange of water in these natural harbours – the bottom may be covered with stagnant water and black mud containing hydrogen sulphide, a colourless, poisonous, rotten-egg-smelling gas that can be used to produce sulphur.

Many fjords dip to astonishingly depths, like Norway's Sognefjorden, which is 1,308 metres deep and stretches for 177 kilometres. Its walls tower 1,000 metres above the water's surface. But Sognefjorden is only the world's second-longest fjord. The longest is located in eastern Greenland, the Nordvest Fjord arm of Scoresbysund, and extends inland from the sea for 314 kilometres.

Fjords are found mainly in Norway, Alaska, Chile, New Zealand, Canada, and Greenland. In some, small streams plunge hundreds of metres over smooth, steep walls, creating some of the world's highest waterfalls. The world's highest sea cliff rises 1,609 metres up from Torssukatak Fjord in southern Greenland.

This iceberg, resembling a small mountain range diagonally sheared across by some seismic convulsion, was formed at Scoresbysund in eastern Greenland. The fjords here are a major source of icebergs, breaking loose from the 'fast ice' of winter and drifting into the shipping lanes, where they pose a hazard to seagoing traffic.

EARTH'S DEEPEST CREVASSE

Antarctic Glacier
Location: East Antarctica
Coordinates: 71° 00' 00" S | 70° 00' 00" E

How low can you go into the heart of a glacier? No one really knows, although a few unfortunate explorers have found out the hard way and never been heard from again.

Crevasses are the deepest openings in a glacier; they are wedge-shaped fractures that typically occur in the upper 50 metres, where the ice is brittle. Below, the ice is more flexible and can slide over uneven surfaces without cracking. Crevasses also occur when different parts of a glacier move at different speeds. For example, when glaciers slide down a valley, the midpoint moves more quickly than the sides, which scrape against the valley's walls. The deepest crevasses ever measured dipped 45 metres below the surface, roughly the height of a 15-story apartment building.

Anywhere a glacier goes – Greenland, Antarctica, Alaska, the Himalaya – a crevasse will follow. Not surprisingly, few explorers are eager to seek out the deepest among them. An educated guess about the location of the world's deepest crevasse leads to Antarctica, where 98 percent of the continent is covered with a thick sheet of ice. Antarctica supports both alpine glaciers, which start in the high basins of mountain ranges and flow down into valleys, and continental glaciers, which simply flow outward. As gravity pulls glaciers and ice sheets downhill, the brittle top layers crack and fracture. Crevasses can "disappear" when blowing snow covers them, which can, in turn, pose invisible hazards to sleds, dogs, and people. The most dangerous crevasses, and most likely the deepest, occur near the coastal and mountainous areas of Antarctica.

Glacial cracks such as this may harbour long-lost remains preserved in the ice. The Oetzi iceman was found in the Italian Alps in 1991, still wearing goatskin leggings and a grass cape, 5,300 years after he was entombed. But science had to wait for the glacier to give him up – and the arrowhead in his shoulder was not discovered for another decade.

EARTH'S LARGEST ICE CAVE

Location: Eisriesenwelt, Austria
Coordinates: 47° 31' 00" N | 13° 10' 00" E

The Eisriesenwelt (literally, "the world of the ice giants") is a short drive from Salzburg, Austria, but once inside it feels like a descent into the deepest, coldest regions of Earth. The holes and passageways of the Eisriesenwelt were carved by an ancient river that left pits and depressions in the land. Over eons, thawing snow and rainwater drained through the limestone bedrock into the caves. Today, it's said that this sprawling underground world actually breathes. In winter, cold air blows into the corridors, freezing the water from melting snow that has dripped into the caves during the warmer months. In summer, a cold breeze flows towards the entrance from within and prevents the ice from melting.

The caves were discovered in 1879 and charted in 1913. Seven years later, with the addition of stairs and walkways, they were opened to the public. Even though this glacial underworld now attracts about 200,000 visitors annually, little more than 1 kilometre of the caves' 42 kilometres of passageways and chambers is accessible to visitors.

The ice in the caverns near the entrance reaches a thickness of 20 metres, and the halls inside contain fantastic ice formations, gigantic columns and towers of ice, ice waterfalls, and glaciers. One structure looks like an elephant, and others are likened to cathedrals and thrones. Ice layers coloured by minerals in the water and by centuries of freezing and thawing make for a lovely frigid mosaic. Portions of this subterranean ice palace carry names from Norse mythology. The imagery here makes the nomenclature seem, even if geographically improbable, entirely apt.

Ice caves originate when water flows through large ice masses, carving out hollows. During the summer, melting water gravitates to the cracks and faults of the glacier which widen and deepen over time. The ice cave above is in California's Sequoia National Park; the ice cave shown on the following page is found in the Perito Moreno glacier in Los Glaciares National Park in Argentina.

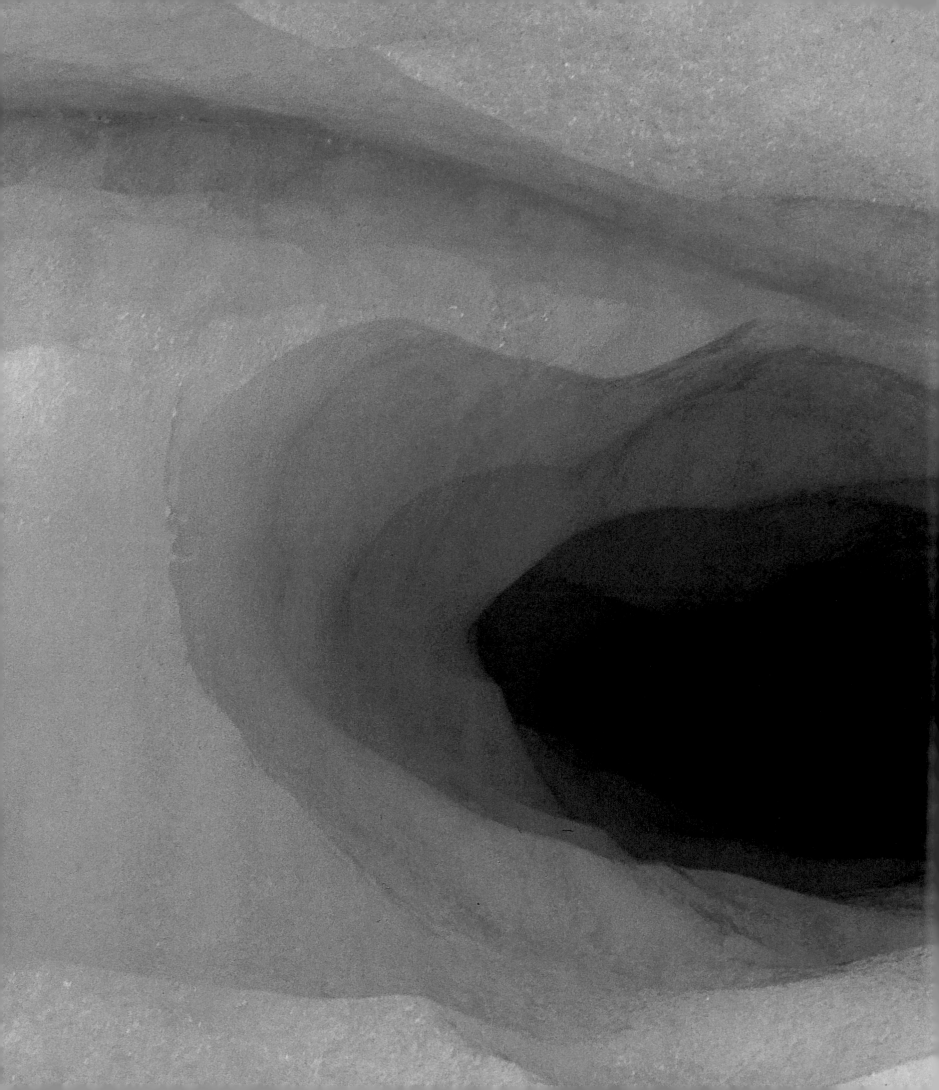

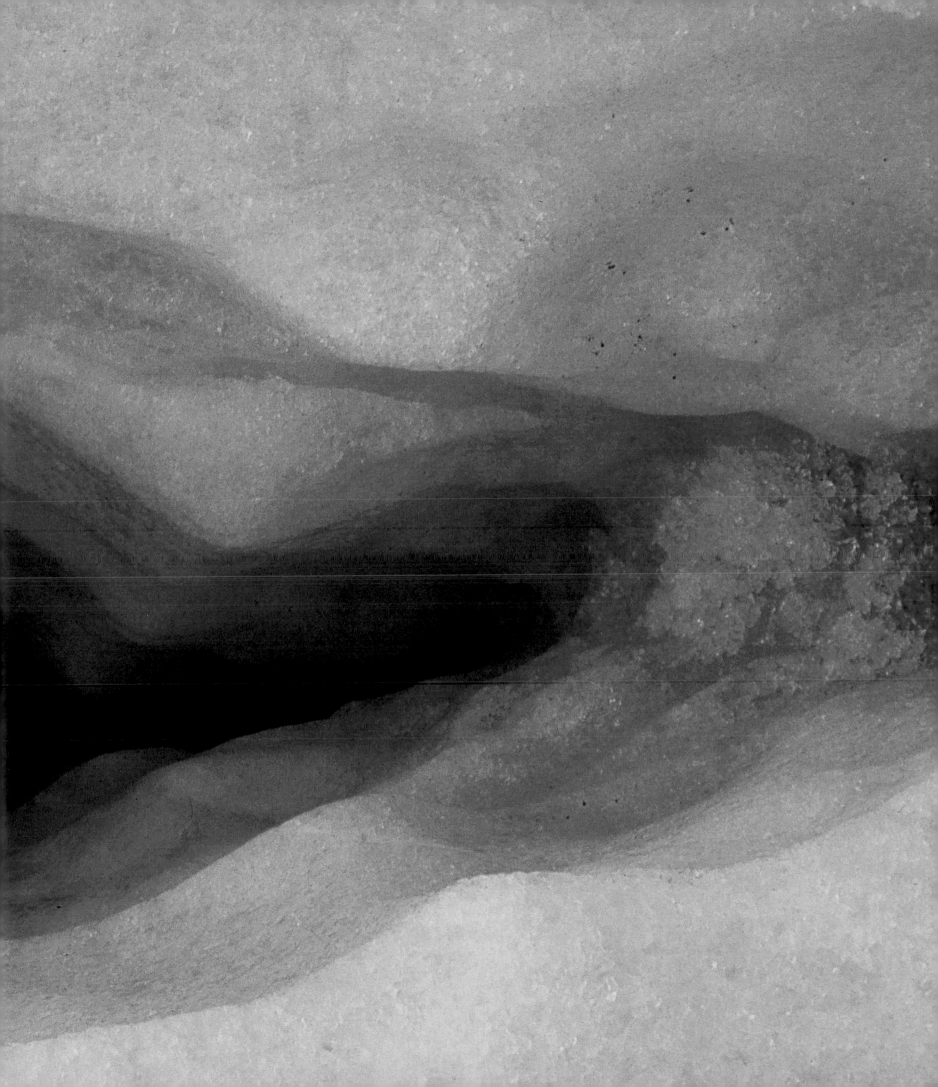

EARTH'S LARGEST SALT FLAT

Salar de Uyuni
Location: Central Bolivia
Total Area: 17,480 km^2
Coordinates: 20° 20′ 00″ S | 67° 42′ 00″ W

Thick, hard crusts of salt form the desiccated crust of Bolivia's Salar de Uyuni, the world's largest salt plain. Exploring this magnificently white landscape, whether by foot or by truck, is like landing on another planet.

Under brilliant sunshine, you might imagine that you're in the Antarctic, crossing a vast tract of ice or snow. Under a full moon, it's easy to think that the abundance of reflected light is anything but natural, that you're in some sort of Martian car park. During the rainy season, between December and April, large tracts are covered with water and become giant mirrors reflecting the chains of mountains that fringe the horizon.

Across the Salar de Uyuni, which is 3,665 metres high, water rarely soaks down more than 1 metre; the salt, however, is packed in layers almost 120 metres deep. Somehow in the rainy season this odd and salty ecosystem still manages to support cacti, flamingos, and rabbit-like *vischacas*. Geologists believe that the Salar de Uyuni occupies what was once the deepest part of an ancient lake, Lago Tauca, which covered this region as recently as 12,000 years ago.

In the 17th century the silver mines on the nearby Cerro Rico, a red-rock, barren peak, were dubbed the 'mouth of hell' by Spanish colonial rulers.

Two conical hills of salt on the Bolivian Salar de Unuyi flats are reflected in the surface of a temporary lake. Salt is vital to life, a staple of trade long before Bolivia exported coca. Even here, in this seeming desert of salinity, life thrives

EARTH'S LOWEST SURFACE POINT

Dead Sea
Location: Israel-Jordan border
403 m below sea level
Coordinates: 31° 30' 00" N | 35° 30' 00" E

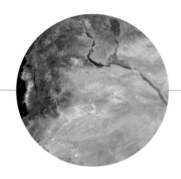

The surface of the Dead Sea is about as deep as the Empire State Building is tall, and its waters are among the world's saltiest – six times saltier than the ocean and too briny to sustain plants, seaweed, or fish. What the Dead Sea does support, however, is mineral-production companies (harvesting mainly potash and bromine) and tourist spas. Bathers come for the water's buoyancy – it's possible to sit on the sea and read a newspaper – and for the health benefits of Dead Sea salts. Because the Dead Sea is located in a hot, dry desert, it loses much of its water through evaporation and over the last 40 years, it has fallen 11 metres. The decline continues.

For the biblically curious, the ancient cities of Sodom and Gomorrah are believed to have been located on the Dead Sea's south-west shore, but visitors will have to use their imagination to find them. Because of its low elevation and low humidity, the area's climate proved ideal for preserving the ancient paper records that came to be known as the Dead Sea Scrolls. In 1947, young Bedouin shepherds found several jars in a cave filled with manuscripts dating from the 3rd century B.C.E. to 68 C.E. This is the same period when Jesus of Nazareth lived, and the scrolls turned out to be almost 1,000 years older than any other surviving manuscripts of the Hebrew scriptures.

Fed by the River Jordan in the north and by springs and streams east and west, the Dead Sea has no outlet, losing vast amounts of water by evaporation. Salt concentration is six times higher than the ocean's.

EARTH'S DEEPEST AND OLDEST FRESHWATER LAKE

Lake Baikal
Location: South-east Siberian Russia
Total Size: 1,742 m deep | 31,494 km^3 of freshwater
Coordinates: 54° 00' 00" N | 109° 00' 00" E

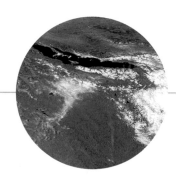

Around the world, even those people who know little about Siberia know that Lake Baikal is our planet's deepest and purest lake. The often-quoted statistics bear repetition.

Lake Baikal's maximum depth is 1,742 metres, and its average depth is 730 metres.

Its mineral content is 96.4 milligrams per litre, compared with at least 400 milligrams for most lakes. In many cases Baikal water can be used instead of distilled water.

Its transparency is 40 metres, 10 times the average.

It contains 20 percent of the world's lake freshwater, equivalent to that of all North America's Great Lakes combined.

Lake Baikal is at least 20 million and possibly 30 million years old. This is the most important statistic. Normally, lakes last no more than 10,000 to 15,000 years before sediments take over. Gradually, floating earth forms a lid, and eventually the lid becomes a bog that may or may not dry out. What limnologists call "its unique physicogeographic characteristics" account for Baikal's diverse and endemic organic life. Fifteen percent of its plants and 60 percent of its animals, out of its more than 2,000 plant and animal species, are found only here.

Even more unfathomable is this observation from Oleg K. Gusev, a biologist, conservationist, and one of Lake Baikal's most eminent defenders: "The deepest point of the lake's rock basin is approximately 7,000 metres below sea level. Its stone bed is the deepest depression in the world, whose 'roots' dissect the whole of the earth's crust, penetrating into the upper mantle to the depth of 50 or 60 kilometres. To put it figuratively, the Baikal depression is a window into the earth's depth, making it possible to understand its [the earth's] inner processes."

Dervla Murphy

Dervla Murphy

BAIKAL

Contemporary travellers tend to meet our world's most precious and irreplaceable lake on two levels: they are fascinated by its physical uniqueness while simultaneously responding to its spiritual significance. In this context, "spiritual" is a tricky word, conveying to some people a sentimental, misty-eyed view of reality. Let's consider pantheism, then, the identification of God with Nature. To many of us, worshipping lakes or trees or mountain summits sounds daft. Yet that mindset recognizes how dependent we human beings are on our natural environment. Modern man glories in his domination of the earth. We fail to see that our contempt for Nature poses the greatest threat to humankind's long-term well-being.

Centuries before scientists recorded its physical uniqueness, the few tribes who lived around Lake Baikal's Siberian shores recognized and revered its magic. They knew it as "the Hallowed Sea". Today the mountainous, roadless coastal hinterlands surrounding the lake still are largely uninhabited, the only dwellings being a few log cabins along the shore used by passing hunters and fishermen.

Not many tourists pass this way either, so I was just one of a few passengers the day I sailed across Lake Baikal to Cape Kotelnikovsky, locally famous for its hot springs. The weather was exceptional for August: an overcast sky and a strong cold wind. But seeing Lake Baikal in this troubled mood, its waves splashing our little boat, allowed intimacy with the water. Midway through the three-hour journey, both shores became invisible, which gave me another clue to Baikal's vastness. Baikal is 400 miles long — an inland sea. What geographers call the Baikal Basin creates its own weather system. It is much windier here than anywhere else in Siberia and slightly less cold in winter because the lake's depth enables it to act as a storage heater.

The hot springs (86°C in all seasons) occupy a beautifully undeveloped clearing surrounded by towering cedars. A score of day-trippers had already arrived, and some were drinking from a covered well, using an enormous, carved wooden ladle. Others were filling plastic bottles, just as devout Roman Catholics do at places of pilgrimage. For millennia Siberia's indigenous tribes have believed in the curative properties of their numerous hot springs for every sort of illness, a belief now shared by Russians of all walks of life.

We continued sailing south for an hour past steep, pathless taiga rising directly from a shore of dark rock. Uneasily I noted the shortage of birds: only a few small colonies of herring gulls appeared all day. Later I learned that industrial development in the Baikal Basin has seriously depleted the lake's bird species.

As we passed chaotic – almost menacing – mountains stretching inland at right angles to the water, past the lichen-covered cliffs of Olkhon, the largest of Baikal's 27 islands, I dipped one hand into its cool waters and thought about epishura. This minute crustacean, peculiar to Baikal, works in teams of millions to eliminate all foreign organic matter, including bones and nonsynthetic garments, from the water. No dead body, human or animal, has ever been recovered from this lake. The epishura keep the water so pure, all the year round, that you can drink it as you swim. There's not a trace of our human presence.

The epishura are crucially important. All the lake's fauna, including the unique Baikal varieties of whitefish, cod, grayling, and seal (the nerpa), depend on them as the first link in their food chain. Epishura can live only in Lake Baikal; even when they are kept in Baikal water in a laboratory, they die. Apart from being an irreplaceable food, they are awesome biological filters. Collaborating with diatomic algae, epishura extract approximately one-quarter million tons of calcium every year from the rivers flowing into Baikal. Thus the lake's saturation with oxygen, even in winter, is entirely dependent on the epishura. It is a tragedy that over the past four decades, the epishura have been dwindling in the southern waters where they are being killed by toxic effluents from the Baikal Paper and Pulp Combine, built some 40 years ago.

For around 25 million years, Lake Baikal gradually evolved, undisturbed and revered as sacred. Then within a few decades, the know-how and greed of 20th-century man has brought it to the verge of disaster. Boris Komarov reminds us that "untouched Siberia is an illusion; industry is devouring its 'green fragile bosom' from all sides, like sulphuric acid, and has already reached is radiant orb – Baikal."

There is, however, still time to save the lake. We all can help by supporting an Irkutsk-based nongovernmental organization for which I have enormous admiration. Baikal Environmental Wave may be contacted at www.baikalwave.eu.org.

EARTH'S LARGEST SALT-WATER LAKE

Caspian Sea
Location: Central Asia
Total Size: 371,000 km²
Coordinates: 42° 00′ 00″ N | 50° 00′ 00″ E

The Caspian Sea is one of those quirks of geographical nomenclature. Even though this Central Asian body of water is landlocked by Azerbaijan, Russia, Kazakhstan, Turkmenistan, and Iran, the ancient Romans, finding it salty, decided it that was a sea and named it *Mare Caspium*. The "Caspian" part of its name comes from the ancient Kaspi people, who once lived in Transcaucasia, to the west. Today, geographers consider the Caspian to be the earth's largest salt-water lake, and the largest inland body of water.

The Caspian contains about one-third of the earth's inland surface water – and its surface area is larger than Japan. It is 28 metres below sea level and reaches a maximum depth of 975 metres. Most of its water comes primarily from the Volga River but the sea has no major outlet.

Curiously, the Caspian hasn't always been the largest salt-water lake in the world. Eleven million years ago it was part of a water chain – including the Sea of Azov, the Black Sea, and the Mediterranean Sea – that linked it to the world's oceans.

At the beginning of the 20th century, the Caspian Sea produced half the world's oil. The fall of the Soviet Union brought economic collapse to the region, but new dreams are being fuelled by increased oil production and a resurgence of oil wealth. Not faring so well are the Caspian's sturgeons, ancient fish that produce 90 percent of the world's caviar but are now threatened by poachers and pollution.

The Caspian may have lost its status as a sea, but locals retain aspirations that can only be described as oceanic. Azerbaijani historian A. K. Bakikhanov set off 150 years ago with two sailboats to find the 'Caspian Atlantis', a fabled set of submerged towns and villages on the lake bed. Others are still excavating today.

EARTH'S HIGHEST LAKE

Licancábur Lake
Location: Northern Chile
Total Size: 5,930 m above sea level
Coordinates: 23° 39′ 00″ S | 70° 24′ 00″ W

Experts can't even agree on the simple definition of a lake, let alone the highest of them. By definition, a lake is a body of water surrounded by land. It can be fresh or salt water, shallow or deep. Once formed, lakes can change dramatically; they can hold their claim to being a lake even if they dry up completely, their basins filling with water only in times of flood.

Lake Titicaca, on the border of Peru and Bolivia in South America, is sometimes considered the world's highest navigable freshwater lake. Both hydrofoil ships and tiny, traditional Indian reed canoes skim across the surface of this 8,290-square-kilometre lake at an elevation of nearly 4 kilometres above sea level.

Other bodies of water claim "highest lake" status. More than a few experts say it is Panch Pokhari, 5,414 metres above sea level on Mount Everest in the Himalaya. There are unnamed glacial lakes even higher on Mount Everest, at 5,886 metres. But these lakes are quite small – Panch Pokhari is slightly more than 2 kilometres long – and they're frozen most of the time.

The strongest contender for the title is the summit-crater lake on top of the 5,930-metre-high extinct volcano Licancábur (right), near Chile's Atacama Desert. Upon closer examination, Licancánbur is a chilly pool with a depth of less than 4 metres that is hiding near the summit of a dormant volcano nearly 6 kilometres high. It accommodates planktonic fauna, "extremophiles", or organisms that thrive in low-oxygen, high-UV-radiation conditions normally considered inhospitable. Interestingly, Licancábur's glacier-free summit holds the remains of an Incan altar and several Incan shelters – an indication of its lure through the ages.

EARTH'S LARGEST FRESHWATER LAKE

Lake Superior
Location: North America
Total Size: 82,414 km²
Coordinates:47° 29′ 58″ N | 88° 00′ 02″ W

North America's five Great Lakes together form Earth's largest body of freshwater and span 247,000 square kilometres, an area bigger than the United Kingdom. Lake Superior is the greatest of the Great Lakes and the world's largest freshwater lake. The name pretty much reveals its geographic significance, but it's also somewhat of a tease.

The first French explorers approached the great inland sea by way of the Ottawa River and Lake Huron, and they referred to their discovery simply as *le lac supérieur*. In translation, the name means "upper lake", or the lake above Lake Huron. These explorers had no idea how huge this lake would turn out to be, but the native Chippewa Indians had a slightly more specific name for the water: Kitchi-gummi, meaning "great water".

Lake Superior's shoreline has high and rocky ledges and dozens of large bays, inlets, and peninsulas, as well as black-sand beaches. It's also the deepest of the Great Lakes, at one point measuring 397 metres deep. About 200 rivers feed this lake, which contains roughly 11 quadrillion litres of water, or enough to flood all of Canada, the United States, Mexico, and South America 30 centimetres deep.

In order of descending size, the Great Lakes chain is composed of Lakes Superior, Huron, Michigan, Ontario, and Erie. Except for Lake Michigan, they provide a natural border between Canada and the United States.

'A lake is the landscape's most beautiful and expressive feature. It is earth's eye; looking into which the beholder measures the depth of his own nature...'

Henry David Thoreau

EARTH'S LARGEST LAKES

1 CASPIAN SEA, NORTH-WEST ASIA | SIZE: 373,000 km² | DEEPEST POINT: 1,025 m
2 LAKE SUPERIOR, NORTH AMERICA | SIZE: 82,414 km² | DEEPEST POINT: 432 m
3 LAKE VICTORIA, AFRICA | SIZE: 69,480 km² | DEEPEST POINT: 89 m
4 LAKE HURON, NORTH AMERICA | SIZE: 59,596 km² | DEEPEST POINT: 250 m
5 LAKE MICHIGAN, NORTH AMERICA | SIZE: 58,016 km² | DEEPEST POINT: 309 m

EARTH'S HOTTEST PLACE UNDER THE OCEAN

Hydrothermal Vents
Location: Mid-Atlantic Ridge
No specific geographic coordinates

Deep beneath the Atlantic Ocean, along the Mid-Atlantic Ridge, which stretches from Iceland to the Antarctic, the ocean floor is constantly oozing magma, creating Earth's newest crust. This vast underwater mountain chain of ridges and valleys is forever spreading, cracking, and giving rise to tall chimney stacks called *black smokers,* which belch out tiny grains of metal sulphides. These black smokers are more formally called *hydrothermal vents*. They are geysers on the seafloor, first discovered in 1977, and are found at an average depth of 2,100 metres. They appear when ocean water seeps into cracks in the cooling rock on the ocean's floor; magma superheats this water, which gurgles back up, building tall mineral chimneys in the process. Water gushing from black smokers can reach a temperature of 400°C, but it doesn't technically boil due to the intense hydrostatic pressure of the ocean's weight. Instead, it rises and cools, releasing minerals and chemicals that sustain nutrient-rich ecosystems where mussels, eyeless shrimp and fish, plants, tube worms, and microorganisms thrive.

The tallest-ever underwater chimney, named Godzilla, was found in the Pacific Ocean off the coast of Oregon. It grew as high as a 15-story building before it toppled.

While black smokers are the hottest of the hydrothermal vents, their cooler cousins are called white smokers. These geological wonders (above) spew out light-coloured barium, calcium, and silicon compounds and they are inhabited by uniquely adapted deep-sea creatures such as blind shrimp and giant tube worms.

EARTH'S PINKEST BODY OF WATER

Lake Natron
Location: Border between Kenya and Tanzania
Total Size: 56 km long | 24 km wide
Coordinates: 02° 30' 00" S | 36° 10' 00" E

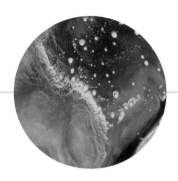

Lake Natron, in Africa's Great Rift Valley, is pink, and it is a soda lake. Hot springs on its floor spurt soda into the pool, and streams from a steep slope surrounding the lake dump more soda into the water. Because Natron has no outlet, all the minerals that pour in stay there. As the alkali salt crust on the surface of the lake becomes concentrated over time, it attracts bacteria by the billions, which feed off the rich mineral base and give the lake its trademark colour. Compounding the light-red glow are the 2.5 million lesser flamingoes that live in the surrounding valley. Lake Natron is the only breeding area for these birds, which feed on spirulina (a blue-green algae with red pigments), because this highly alkaline environment acts as a barrier against predators

trying to reach the birds' nests. Another impediment is the sweltering temperature of the mud, which can reach 50°C beneath Natron's neon waters. Amazingly, the alkaline tilapia, a species of fish endemic to this area, thrives in the waters at the edges of the hot-spring inlets.

The area around the lake is hot and arid but offers spectacular volcanic scenery. Partly because the lake is large, its appearance frequently fluctuates with the changing pattern of its salt crust and the red pigments of the algae and bacteria on the surface. On some days and from some angles, Natron is a brownish soup. But seen in the right light, flying over Natron in a small aeroplane, the lake is bright pink.

Natron, or sesquicarbonate of soda, was used as a drying agent by the ancient Egyptians to prepare the dead for mummification. For the pink flamingo, the salts of Lake Natron – its only breeding ground – play a different protective role: they are so caustic they keep away potential predators from the birds' nests.

THE WHITE LINE IN THE PACIFIC

They say the only thing on Earth that can be seen from space is the Great Wall of China. Untrue! The only Earth phenomenon that astronauts can see is a white line that randomly pops up in the Pacific. Every now and then, in different parts of the ocean, currents well up from the ocean floor, bringing nutrients to the surface. These upwelling currents affect less than 0.1 percent of the ocean's surface, but they provide more than 50 percent of all the fish caught. They also give us a strange, 2-kilometre-wide white line in the Pacific.

The white line was photographed during a 10-year-long international programme called the Joint Global Ocean Flux Study. Scientists wanted to see how various currents and chemicals in the ocean moved around the planet, so they measured factors such as ocean colour, the movement of warm and cold currents, and surface temperature. They used Orion P-3 aircraft flying at an altitude of 150 metres to radiate the water with a weak blue-green laser beam, which made the chlorophyll in the water fluoresce.

One of the photographs taken from the space shuttle shows an almost-straight line in the Pacific Ocean, hundreds of kilometres long. Looking back through ships' records for the past century, scientists found that this temporary line was usually seen between August and January, when cold water loaded with minerals and nutrients swells up from the ocean floor until it hits the surface and then rolls west. At the surface is a zone where a slab of cold water about 70 metres thick dives under a 40-metre-thick slab of warmer water.

The water can be quite turbulent, with breaking whitecaps. There also are patches of pale green water loaded with tiny algae, diatoms called *Rhizosolenia*. These diatoms are about two to three times thicker than a human hair. An ocean explorer in 1926 described them as "so abundant in places they were of the consistency of soup". The colour comes from the combination of the whitecaps, the colder water, and the squillions of diatoms.

When the cold water wells up from the ocean floor, the diatoms pile up just ahead of it as it moves west, and they feed on the water's nutrients. According to the measurements taken by the laser in the low-flying aircraft, these diatoms were 100 times more abundant in the zone between the cold and hot water than elsewhere. But not only were there lots of diatoms having a good feed, they were also having sex once a day: dividing and making baby diatomettes. Once a pool of cold water wells up from the ocean floor, it creates a very localized and a very productive food web that lasts for only a very short time.

So it turns out that a collection of fish, foam, and future fertilizer, when all lined up fighting, feeding and fornicating, are more visible from space than the Great Wall of China.

Dr Karl S. Kruszelnicki

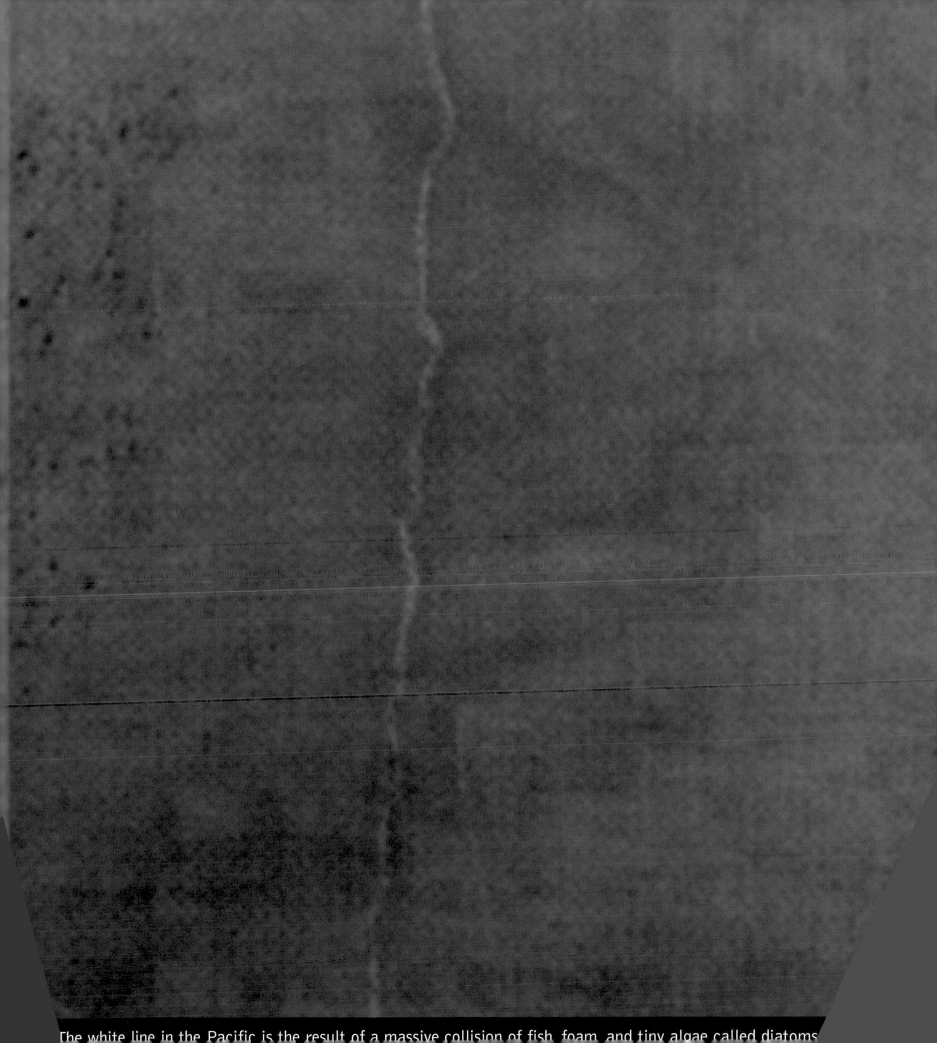

The white line in the Pacific is the result of a massive collision of fish, foam, and tiny algae called diatoms

INDEX

INDEX

CREDITS/ACKNOWLEDGEMENTS

Grateful acknowledgement is made to the following sources and photographers for permission to reproduce their photographs on the following pages:

Anne Alders: 174-5;

Bryan and Cherry Alexander: 157; 165; 276-7

Art Directors and Trip:11 (D.Clegg); 86-7 (C.C); 117 (B. Masters); 129 (J. Arnold); 135 (Eric Smith); 136-7(P. Terry); 139 (Eric Smith); 140-1 (Viesti Collection); 145 (B. Gadsby); 180-1 (Archive Photos); 227 (Ask Images); 253 (M.Jelliffe); 301 (I.Burgandinov)

Auscape: 57 (Jean-Paul Ferrero); 58-9 (Jean-Paul Ferrero); 65 (Jean-Paul Ferrero); 245 (D.Parer and E.Parer-Cook); 246-7 (D.Parer and E.Parer-Cook)

Bruce Coleman: 98-9 (Luiz Claudio Marigo); 216-7 (Pacific Stock); 251 (Atlantic SNC)

Corbis: 31 (Galen Rowell); 67 (Douglas Peebles); 68 (Douglas Peebles); 69 (Bob Krist); 104-5 (Lloyd Cluff); 107 (The Purcell Team); 121 (Jim Sugar); 123 (Galen Rowell); 179 (A.&J.Verkaik); 185 (Listin Diaro); 187 (Sygma); 189 (Rob Matheson); 210 left; 210 right; 211; 236-7 (Roger Ressmeyer); 257 (Steve Raymer); 261 (K.M.Westermann); 263 (Liang Zhuoming); 309 (Ralph White)

Kevin Downey: 77 (Urs Widmer)

Evergreen Photo Alliance: 113 (Boyd Norton)

FLPA: 22-3 (Minden Pictures); 29 (Keith Rushforth); 44-5 (David Hosking); 94-5 (Winfried Wisniewski); 213 (G.P.Eaton); 215 (Panda Photo); 230 (USDA); 231 (USDA); 281 (Steve McCutcheon); 305 (Larry West)

Getty: 291 (Art Wolfe)

Images of Africa Photobank: 311 (David Keith Jones)

Doranne Jacobson: 163

Lonely Planet: Images: 47 (Diana Mayfield); 83 (Richard Cummins); 103 (Matt Fletcher); 125 (Michael Aw); 166-7 (David Tipling); 243 (Greg Johnston); 275 (Ralph Lee Hopkins)

Mountain Camera: 15 (Colin Monteath); 21 (John English); 27 (John Cleare); 75 (John Cleare)

NASA: 149; 313

Naturepl.com: 35 (Giles Bracher); 37 (David Welling); 39 (David Welling); 49 (Hugh Maynard); 71 (Jeff Foott); 97 (Staffan Widstrand); 101 (Rhonda Klevansky); 111 (Arup Shah); 119 (Martha Holmes); 127 (Jeff Foott); 130-1 (Neil Lucas); 133 (Dave Watts); 151 (Jorma Luhta); 229 (Jurgen Freund); 232-3 (Michael Pitts); 239 (AFLO); 255 (Hanne & Jens Ericksen); 287 (David Welling); 293 (Nigel Bean); 303 (Doug Allan)

NHPA: 63 (Daniel Heuclin); 197 (K.Ghani); 285 (Alberto Nardi)

Oxford Scientific Films: 81 (Adam Jones); 91 (Tony Martin); 108-9 (Owen Newman); 152-3 (Olivier Grunewald); 155 (Warren Faidley); 169 (Tui de Roy); 171 (Mary Plage); 207 (Ronald Toms); 219 (Mary Plage); 225 (Richard Packwood); 267 (Konrad Woche); 268-9 (Alastair MacEwan); 273 (Norbert Rosing); 295 (Doug Allan); 298-9 (Martyn Colbeck)

Tom Pfeiffer: 201; 202; 203; 205; 208-9

Janusz Rosiek: 33

Science Photo Library: 72-3 (Adam Jones)

Still Pictures: 19 (Galen Rowell); 43 (Klein/Hubert); 50-1 (Dick Ross); 55 (Klein/Hubert); 115 (Lineair); 161 (Philippe Henry); 183 (Nigel Dickinson); 195 (Michael Gunther); 198-9 (Robert Mackinlay); 221 (D.Decobecq); 249 (Andy Camp); 265 (Andre Bartschi); 288-9 (Alan Watson)

Woodfall Wild Images: 53 (Martin Zwick); 79 (Nigel Hicks); 93 (Andreas Leeman); 271 (David Woodfall); 279 (Steve Austin); 283 (Steve Austin)

CONTRIBUTORS' BIOGRAPHIES

GEORGE C. BAND was, at the age of 23, the youngest member of Sir Edmund Hillary's famous expedition to the top of Mt. Everest in 1953. Two years later, he was the first to climb Kangchenjunga, the world's third-highest peak. His new book, *Everest: 50 Years at the Top of the World*, commemorates the 50th anniversary of the Everest achievement.

SIR RANULPH FIENNES was named the "World's Greatest Living Explorer" by the *Guinness Book of Records*. His expeditions include the first surface journey around the world's polar axis; the Anglo Soviet North Pole Expedition; and the longest unsupported journey across the South Pole. He lives in England.

SEBASTIAN JUNGER is an award-winning journalist and the best-selling author of *The Perfect Storm* and *Fire*. He has been drawn to "extreme situations and people at the edges of things" since childhood and is currently reporting on war, terrorism and human rights from embattled regions across the world. He lives in New York City and Cape Cod, Massachusetts.

DR. KARL KRUSZELNICKI is Australia's most beloved popular science writer and media personality. He has published 20 books, the most recent of which is *Why It Is So: Headless Chickens, Bathroom Queues and Belly Button Blues*. He is the Julius Sumner Miller Fellow at the University of Sydney.

ELLEN MACARTHUR earned international accolades when she sailed around the world, finishing second in the 2000-2001 Vendée Globe. Her recent book, *Taking on the World,* recounted her dramatic experience at sea as well as her own life story.

PATRICIA MOEHLMAN is a behavioural ecologist who has spent most of her work life in Africa studying the animals of the Serengeti Plain. She earned the nickname "Jackal Woman" at the beginning of her career while studying the wild dogs in Tanzania in the late 1960s and 1970s. She still works in East Africa, but now has also become extensively involved in conservation efforts, working with native populations to ensure that threatened wild animals get the protection they need.

Since 1964 DERVLA MURPHY has written 20 books about her extraordinary travels. She has cycled across from Dunkirk to New Delhi, travelled with a mule through the Simien mountains in Ethiopia, and walked from Kajamarca to Cuzco, Peru. Her next book is on eastern Siberia. She lives in Ireland.

DR. HARALDUR SIGURDSSON has been a professor at the Graduate School of Oceanography, University of Rhode Island, since 1974. As one of the world's leading vulcanologists, he is the author of *Melting the Earth: The Evolution of Ideas about Volcanic Eruptions*.

GEORGE W. STONE is an editor at National Geographic Traveler, for which he writes frequently about a wide range of topics. He is also involved with efforts to clamp down on child exploitation globally.

SARA WHEELER is one of the world's most esteemed travel journalists. Her book, *Terra Incognita*, which tells the story of seven months in Antarctica, became an international bestseller. Other books include *Travels in a Thin Country*, the story of a journey through Chile, and *Cherry: A Life of Apsley Cherry-Garrard*, a biography of the youthful sledger on Captain Scott's team who went on to write the polar classic *The Worst Journey in the World*. She is currently writing about British East Africa and Denys Finch Hatton, the English aristocrat famously played by Robert Redford in the Hollywood epic *Out of Africa*.

SIMON WINCHESTER is a trained geologist, world traveller, and the author of 20 books including the international best sellers *The Map That Changed the World* and *The Professor and the Madman*. His newest work is *Krakatoa: The Day the World Exploded*. He lives in New York City.

'To cherish what remains of the Earth and to foster its renewal is our only legitimate hope of survival'

Wendell Berry